Move on Maths!
Ages 9–11

Move on Maths!

The *Move on Maths!* series presents fun, versatile, tried and tested maths resources for years 3, 4, 5 and 6 which you can use in the way that is most suitable for your pupils. The units offer flexible ideas which can be used for maths lessons or homework, and support the Renewed Primary Framework for Mathematics. The PNS Framework objectives are clearly shown for every sheet, followed by unit learning outcomes, so it's easy to choose the right worksheet to suit you and your children's needs.
Also available:

Move on Maths! 7–9 Years
50+ flexible maths activities
John Taylor

Move on Maths! Ages 9–11

50+ flexible maths activities

John Taylor

Routledge
Taylor & Francis Group
LONDON AND NEW YORK

First published 2009
by Routledge
2 Park Square, Milton Park, Abingdon, Oxon OX14 4RN

Simultaneously published in the USA and Canada
by Routledge
270 Madison Avenue, New York, NY 10016

Routledge is an imprint of the Taylor & Francis Group, an informa business

© 2009 Robert John Taylor

Typeset in Frutiger by Wearset Ltd, Boldon, Tyne and Wear
Printed and bound in Great Britain by
MPG Books Ltd, Bodmin

British Library Cataloguing in Publication Data
A catalogue record for this book is available from the British Library

Library of Congress Cataloging-in-Publication Data
Taylor, John, 1953–
    Move on maths! Ages 9–11: 50+ flexible maths activities/John Taylor.
        p. cm.
    1. Mathematics—Study and teaching (Elementary)—Activity programs. I. Title. II. Title: 50+ flexible maths activities. III. Title: Fifty plus flexible maths activities.
    QA135.6.T358 2009
    372.7–dc22   2008046074

ISBN10: 0-415-47154-0 (pbk)
ISBN13: 978-0-415-47154-1 (pbk)

Contents

Measurement

Handling Data

Acknowledgements

I would like to thank illustrator Sarah Glenn who has provided drawings for the worksheets. The worksheet exercises were previously printed as part of the Maths Express series published by Ginn.

Introduction

About this book

Move on Maths! Ages 9–11 is a flexible teaching resource, designed to help you with implementation of the renewed Primary Framework for Mathematics in your Year 5 and Year 6 classroom and meet the needs of your students.

The book is complemented by *Move on Maths! Ages 7–9*, a teaching resource for Year 3 and Year 4 that follows the same structure.

Supporting the renewed Framework

This practical workbook provides you with learning material that will enable your students to practise key mathematical principles and practice identified by the Framework. It gives you 32 units for Year 5 and 28 units for Year 6, and these offer you a bank of exercises, examples and activities that can be slotted easily into your lesson planning or given to your students as homework.

The units are organised into four sections, which are designed to broaden and develop understanding of the four key Framework strands:

A   Using and **A**pplying Mathematics
S   Understanding **S**hape
M   **M**easuring
D   Handling **D**ata

Organisation of the book

The user-friendly format of the book makes it easy to find the appropriate unit with support information, activity suggestions and worksheet answers alongside.

Each section is subdivided into resources for Year 5 (ages 9–10) and Year 6 (ages 10–11). The print masters are numbered using the strand letter (A, S, M or D) followed by the year group and the worksheet number. For example M5/2 is the second Year 5 sheet in the Measuring strand. These numbers are printed as 'thumb tabs' on the right-hand edge of the page.

The Using and Applying Mathematics sections can be used to test if pupils can apply specific skills that have been taught.

Unit structure

Each unit is designed around a learning objective from the Framework and contains a *Student photocopiable worksheet* and *Teachers' notes*.

Teachers' notes

These are printed alongside a page of corresponding *Student photocopiable worksheet* and include:

- Learning objective from the Framework
- Notes on prior knowledge and skills that are required
- Suggestions for starter activities and games for group work
- Answers to the worksheet questions.

While the student worksheets are designed to be written on and filled in by your students, the Teachers' notes will support you in introducing the topic, and guide you through the prior knowledge your students need to have in order to do the worksheet exercises. They will also give you plenty of ideas for starter activities to get your class stuck in to the topic you are asking them to practise in the worksheets.

Student photocopiable worksheets

These practical sheets will give your students plenty of practice in the key mathematical skills and principles. They are designed to accelerate progress through the learning objectives identified in the Teachers' notes.

The sheets provide a wealth of fun exercises, examples and problems for your students to tackle either as part of your main maths lessons, or as their homework. They are written with differentiation in mind: the *challenge sections* that appear in some exercises will support the needs of your more able students.

Their structure is student-friendly and designed to enhance mathematical learning. The worksheets contain the following:

- Quick introduction to the topic that shows the student how to do the exercises
- Drawing to help the students (selected worksheets)
- Questions, exercises and problems to consolidate learning
- Challenge section that contains more difficult exercises and is designed to stretch the more able students.

Unit A5/1 Problems with negative and positive numbers and time intervals

PNS Framework objectives

- Represent a puzzle or problem by identifying and recording the information or calculations needed to solve it; find possible solutions and confirm them in the context of the problem.
- Count from any given number in whole-number and decimal steps, extending beyond zero when counting backwards; relate the numbers to their position on a number line.

Unit learning outcome

- To apply knowledge to problems with negative and positive numbers and time intervals.

Prior knowledge

- Able to count forwards and back.
- Able to count past zero from positive to negative numbers and vice versa.

Starter activities

- Play 'Frog Jump!'.
- On the whiteboard draw a series of lily pads numbered 0 to 20, BUT leave space to the left of the zero pad so that more can be added to the left later. Announce that the object is to see how many goes it will take to get a frog from the start (the zero lily pad) to a nominated pad. Stick a cut-out frog on the zero lily pad. A dice will be thrown to decide how many lily pads it jumps in each go. Move the cut-out frog accordingly.
- When the frog overshoots its target introduce a second, differently coloured dice to be thrown with the first one to decide if the frog should jump backwards or forwards – back if it shows an odd number.
- Inevitably, backward jumps will bring the frog back beyond zero – what can we do? Insert extra lily pads to the left of zero, numbered −1, −2, etc.
- Vary the game by changing the starting point and the target, including using lily pads with negative numbers.

Answers to A5/1

	(a)	(b)	(c)	(d)	(e)	(f)
1	−14°C	−30°C	−38°C	1°C	6°C	−35°C
2	9 mins	6 mins	3 mins	9 mins	9 mins	9 mins
3	10 days	12 days	26 days	15 days	32 days	1068 years

Unit A5/1 Problems with negative and positive numbers and time intervals

1   On Christmas Eve the temperature outside Father Christmas's house is −24° Celsius.
     What will it be if it:
     (a)   rises 10 degrees? ....
     (b)   falls 6 degrees? ....
     (c)   falls 14 degrees? ....
     (d)   rises 25 degrees? ....
     (e)   rises 30 degrees? ....
     (f)   falls 11 degrees? ....

2   A train is supposed to arrive at the station at 09:00 each morning and leave 2 minutes
     later. It usually leaves late.
     How long does it spend in the station if it arrives and leaves at these times?
     (a)   Monday: arrives 5 minutes early and leaves 2 minutes late   .... minutes
     (b)   Tuesday: arrives 1 minute early and leaves 3 minutes late   .... minutes
     (c)   Wednesday: arrives 2 minutes late and leaves 3 minutes late   .... minutes
     (d)   Thursday: arrives 3 minutes early and leaves 4 minutes late   .... minutes
     (e)   Friday: arrives 6 minutes early and leaves 1 minute late   .... minutes
     (f)   Saturday: arrives 8 minutes early and leaves 1 minute early   .... minutes

3   Calculate the interval between:
     (a)   4 days before 1st April and 6 days after ....
     (b)   8 days before 16th May and 4 days after ....
     (c)   10 days before 2nd August and 16 days after ....
     (d)   7 days before Christmas Day and 8 days after ....
     (e)   12 days before 1st January and 20 days after ....
     (f)   2 BC and AD 1066 ....

Unit A5/2 Problems with triangular numbers

PNS Framework objective

- Explore patterns, properties and relationships and propose a general statement involving numbers or shapes; identify examples for which the statement is true or false.

Unit learning outcome

- To explore problems with triangular and square numbers.

Prior knowledge

- Competent with using pencil and paper calculations.
- Knowledge of square numbers.

Starter activities

- Use large, non-connecting cubes to make stacks in either of these layouts:

 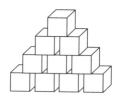

  Make stacks with 2, 3, 4, 5 and 6 rows. Count up the number of cubes in each stack and look at the sequence. Can you work out how many cubes would be needed to make stacks of 7, 8, 9 and 10 rows?

- Use connecting cubes to make layers for a pyramid using square numbers for each layer: 1, 4, 9, 16, 25. NOTE: when connecting the cubes, do so without any of the 'male' connectors protruding.

  Like this 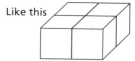 Not like this

  Build up the pyramid by placing the 16 cubes on top of the 25, the 9 on the 16 and so on. How many cubes are there in the top layer, top two layers, etc.? How many cubes would be needed to make a pyramid with 6, 7 or 8 layers?

- Use non-connecting cubes to build a pyramid.

Answers to A5/2

1	(a)	36 boxes	(b)	55 boxes			
2	(a)	49 boxes	(b)	40 boxes	(c)	34 boxes	
3	(a)	14 tins	(b)	30 tins	(c)	55 tins	(d)	91 tins
	(e)	140 tins	(f)	204 tins	(g)	285 tins	(h)	385 tins

Unit A5/2 Problems with triangular numbers

1 Kevin the supermarket shelf-stacker is trying to impress his boss.

He stacks boxes of chocolates in layers of 8, 7, 6, 5, 4, 3, 2 and 1 box on the top layer.

(a) How many boxes of chocolates does he fit in the stack? ....

(b) He adds two more layers, 9 and 10 boxes. How many boxes are in the stack now? ....

2 He notices the boxes at the bottom starting to squash.

How many boxes will be left in the stack if he removes:

(a) the top 3 layers? ....

(b) the top 5 layers? ....

(c) the top 6 layers? ....

3 Kevin has a try at making a square pyramid with tins of cat food. Each layer is a square number.

How many tins will he need for:

(a) 3 layers? ....

(b) 4 layers? ....

(c) 5 layers? ....

(d) 6 layers? ....

(e) 7 layers? ....

(f) 8 layers? ....

(g) 9 layers? ....

(h) 10 layers? ....

Unit A5/3 Problems with metric units of measure

PNS Framework objectives

- Plan and pursue an enquiry; present evidence by collecting, organising and interpreting information; suggest extensions to the enquiry.
- Read, choose, use and record standard metric units to estimate and measure length, weight and capacity to a suitable degree of accuracy (e.g. the nearest centimetre); convert larger to smaller units using decimals to one place (e.g. change 2.6 kg to 2600 g).

Unit learning outcome

- To solve problems with metric units of measure involving conversion to common units.

Prior knowledge

- Knowledge of metric units of length, area and mass.
- Able to use place value to convert units.

Starter activity

- Brainstorm items that might be bought for a house and a garden, and use a Carroll diagram to sort how the items are likely to be measured (e.g. house: carpet, food items, curtain fabric; garden: paving slabs, sand, garden hose, seeds, turf, etc.).

	Length	Area	Weight
House			
Garden			

Sort the suggestions according to which units of measure are likely to be used: mm, cm or m; cm² or m²; g, kg or tonnes. Which measurements are likely to be the most accurate?

Answers to A5/3

1 (a) Measurements of length (given in any order): 180 cm, 7240 mm, 643.5 cm, 5.8 m, 5678 cm, 0.25 km, 976 mm, 2.5 m
Measurements of area (any order): 2.4 m², 10 825 cm², 0.2 m², 951 m², 4325 cm², 210 m²
   (b) 0.976 m, 1.8 m, 2.5 m, 5.8 m, 6.435 m, 7.24 m, 56.78 m, 250 m
   (c) 210 m², 0.2 m² (2000 cm²), 4325 cm², 10 825 cm², 2.4 m² (24 000 cm²), 951 m² (9 510 000 cm²)

2 (a) Measurements of length (any order): 2525 cm, 70 m, 365 m, 8.5 m, 9.99 m, 7350 mm, 77 mm, 99.9 cm
Measurements of weight (any order): 3 tonnes, 560 kg, 3 kg, 500 g, 0.75 kg, 0·5 tonnes, 5000 kg, 600 g
   (b) 77 mm, 99.9 cm, 365 cm, 7350 mm, 8.5 m, 9.99 m, 2525 cm, 70 m
   (c) 5000 kg, 3 tonnes, 560 kg, 0.5 tonnes, 3 kg, 0.75 kg, 600 g, 500 g

Unit A5/3 Problems with metric units of measure

1   Colin got a job as a trainee surveyor. He had to measure lengths and areas. He used the back of an envelope. And got his measurements muddled up.

(a)   Sort out his measurements into:

measurements of length: ....

measurements of area: ....

(b)   Change the length measurements into metres and list them in order, starting with the shortest.

....

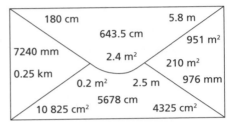

180 cm   5.8 m
643.5 cm
951 m²
7240 mm   2.4 m²
210 m²
0.25 km
0.2 m²   2.5 m   976 mm
5678 cm
10 825 cm²   4325 cm²

(c)   List the area measurements in order, starting with the smallest.
Reminder: 1 m² (square metre) = 10 000 cm² (square centimetres).

....

2   Colin's next job is selling building materials but he still gets confused.

(a)   Sort out his measurements into

measurements of length:

....

....

measurements of weight:

....

....

BODGIT Building Suppliers

3 tonnes   77 mm   70 m

2525 cm   3 kg   9.99 m

0.75 kg   0.5 tonnes

8.5 m   5000 kg   365 cm

600 g   560 kg

99.9 cm

7350 mm   500 g

(b)   List the length measurements in order, starting with the shortest length.

....

(c)   Put the weight measurements in order, starting with the heaviest.
Reminder: 1 tonne = 1000 kg.   ....

Unit A5/4 Interpreting frequency charts

PNS Framework objectives

- Represent a puzzle or problem by identifying and recording the information or calculations needed to solve it; find possible solutions and confirm them in the context of the problem.
- Answer a set of related questions by collecting, selecting and organising relevant data; draw conclusions, using ICT to present features, and identify further questions to ask.

Unit learning outcome

- To identify the functions necessary to solve problems involving frequency charts.

Prior knowledge

- Able to identify the correct data and operations to answer specific questions.
- Competent with addition and subtraction involving HTUs.

Starter activity

- 'Computation race 1': Start by throwing three dice and write the results on the whiteboard – ask children what the highest number is that they can make from the three digits. Throw the dice again and find the smallest number. All together, add the two numbers together and subtract the larger from the smaller.

  Divide the children into groups of three to five, each with a supply of scrap paper. For each round throw the three dice twice for two sets of digits. Each group has to work together to find the two answers, and bring them (and their group name/number) to you on a piece of paper.

  You keep them in the order in which they are received. Work out the correct answers and award points to the groups with both correct answers, giving maximum points to the first correct group and fewer points to the other groups according to the order in which they brought their answers.

Answers to A5/4

1 (a) Monday and Wednesday (b) Saturday (c) 441 (d) 427 (e) 21
2 (a) Monday (b) Wednesday (c) Monday (d) Friday (e) Monday
(f) Monday (g) Wednesday and Thursday (h) Friday

Unit A5/4 Interpreting frequency charts

1   A local ice-cream parlour has introduced some new products and is keeping a check on the sales.

	Mon	Tue	Wed	Thur	Fri	Sat
Grape-flavoured lolly	548	685	541	542	681	968
Tomato-flavoured lolly	6	18	13	25	19	27

(a)   Which day has the least sales? ....

(b)   Which day has the most sales? ....

(c)   What is the difference between the best sales day and the worst? ....

(d)   What is the difference between the best and worst days for grape-flavoured lolly sales day? ....

(e)   What is the difference between the best and worst days for tomato-flavoured lolly sales day? ....

2   As part of a road-safety project the council is counting traffic passing a school for 1 hour before and after school.

		Mon	Tue	Wed	Thur	Fri
Morning	Cars and small vans	745	634	368	487	586
	Large vans and lorries	254	176	284	165	134
Afternoon	Cars and small vans	557	495	378	269	251
	Large vans and lorries	356	312	188	205	85

(a)   Which day is busiest for cars and small vans? ....

(b)   Which day is quietest for cars and small vans? ....

(c)   Which day is busiest for large vans and lorries? ....

(d)   Which day is quietest for large vans and lorries? ....

(e)   Which day has the busiest morning traffic? ....

(f)   Which day has the busiest afternoon traffic? ....

(g)   Which day has the quietest morning traffic? ....

(h)   Which day has the quietest afternoon traffic? ....

Unit A5/5 Problems with addition of groups of numbers

PNS Framework objectives

- Represent a puzzle or problem by identifying and recording the information or calculations needed to solve it; find possible solutions and confirm them in the context of the problem.
- Use a calculator to solve problems, including those involving decimals or fractions (e.g. find $\frac{3}{4}$ of 150 g); interpret the display correctly in the context of measurement.

Unit learning outcome

- To use the appropriate function to solve a variety of problems involving addition of groups of numbers.

Prior knowledge

- Able to identify the correct data to answer specific questions.
- Competent with addition involving HTUs.

Starter activity

- 'Computation race 2': This is organised in the same way as 'Computation race 1' (described in notes for A5/4). For each round throw the three dice twice, pausing in between to write down the first set of numerals before throwing a second time. Each group has to arrange each set of numerals into the highest number possible then add both numbers together. When done they rush their written answer and their working out to you.

Answers to A5/5

1   Totals: 68 infant tables, 74 junior tables, 114 infant chairs, 92 junior chairs, 51 adult chairs, 47 small cupboards, 18 large cupboards, 27 sets of shelves

Nursery:	13 tables,	20 chairs,	12 cupboards
Reception:	21 tables,	37 chairs,	8 cupboards
Class 1:	22 tables,	36 chairs,	8 cupboards
Class 2:	20 tables,	29 chairs,	8 cupboards
Class 3:	15 tables,	35 chairs,	7 cupboards
Class 4:	16 tables,	36 chairs,	5 cupboards
Class 5:	18 tables,	31 chairs,	8 cupboards
Class 6:	17 tables,	33 chairs,	9 cupboards

2   Altogether there are:

474 pencil crayons, 450 folders, 301 ballpoint pens, 180 felt-tip pens, 106 red pens, 149 blue pens, 61 black pens, 481 pens altogether, 75 pairs of children's scissors, 20 pairs of adults' scissors

Unit A5/5 Problems with addition of groups of numbers

The headteacher of Priory School has spent too long on paperwork and has finally gone completely mad.

He has decided to count the furniture, '... just in case a meteor lands on the school.'

	'Infant' tables	'Junior' tables	'Infant' chairs	'Junior' chairs	Adult chairs	Small cupboards	Large cupboards	Sets of shelves
Nursery	12	1	18		2	8	4	5
Reception	18	3	32	2	3	6	2	3
Class 1	20	2	35		1	7	1	6
Class 2	12	8	20	7	2	5	3	4
Class 3	4	11	8	26	1	5	2	2
Class 4	2	14	1	32	3	4	1	3
Class 5		18		17	14	6	2	2
Class 6		17		8	25	6	3	2
Totals								

1   Fill in his totals on the table above and complete the details for each class:

Nursery has   .... tables, ... chairs and .... cupboards.

Reception has .... tables, ... chairs and .... cupboards.

Class 1 has   .... tables, ... chairs and .... cupboards.

Class 2 has   .... tables, ... chairs and .... cupboards.

Class 3 has   .... tables, ... chairs and .... cupboards.

Class 4 has   .... tables, ... chairs and .... cupboards.

Class 5 has   .... tables, ... chairs and .... cupboards.

Class 6 has   .... tables, ... chairs and .... cupboards.

2   He spent last Friday hiding in the stockroom instead of going to a headteachers' meeting and did more counting!

Altogether there are:

.... pencil crayons

.... folders

.... ballpoint pens

.... felt-tip pens

.... red pens

.... blue pens

.... black pens

.... pens altogether

.... pairs of children's scissors   .... pairs of adults' scissors

Pencil crayons		Scissors		Folders		Pens	
Black	37	Adults'		Blue	5	Ballpoint red	49
Blue	34	Good quality	2	Cream	187	Ballpoint blue	63
Green	157	Poor quality	13	Green	25	Ballpoint black	24
Orange	83	Bent and broken	5	Grey	153	Ballpoint green	165
Purple	53			Orange	37	Fine felt black	37
Red	38	Children's		Red	29	Fine felt blue	86
Yellow	72	Left-handed	48	Yellow	14	Fine felt red	57
		Right-handed	27				

Unit A5/6 Problems involving division with remainders

PNS Framework objectives

- Solve one-step and two-step problems involving whole numbers and decimals and all four operations, choosing and using appropriate calculation strategies, including calculator use.
- Extend mental methods for whole-number calculations, for example, to multiply a two-digit by a one-digit number (e.g. 12 × 9), to multiply by 25 (e.g. 16 × 25), to subtract one near-multiple of 1000 from another (e.g. 6070 − 4097).

Unit learning outcome

- To decide which function(s) are needed to problems involving division with remainders.

Prior knowledge

- Able to use conventional notation to carry out division with remainders.

Starter activities

- Play the 'Division race'.

  How to play: Pupils sit in groups around a table, with 50 cubes (or other sorting objects) in the centre. You call out a number that the cubes must be sorted into. The first group to sort them into sets and declare how many sets and how many remaining wins a point. After a few tries increase the number of cubes each group has.

- Play 'Join Up 1' (as per *Jumpstart! Numeracy*, John Taylor, David Fulton Publishers)

  How to play: This game requires an open area that allows free movement, ideally a school hall.

  The children walk freely about, perhaps in a style you specify (e.g. *creeping into the house without waking anyone, like a giant with a headache*). As soon as you shout out a number they each have to get into a group of that number and sit down. Children who are without a group are eliminated and decide with you which number to call out next by choosing a number that is not a factor of the number of children remaining in the game. If a group of the wrong number of children sits down they are also eliminated. The survivors resume their movement. Play continues until you are down to the last two or three children.

Answers to A5/6

1 (a) 40 (b) 30 (c) 24 (d) 20 (e) 17 (f) 15 (g) size E
2 (a) 36 boots (b) 9 pairs (c) 3 (d) 33 (e) 9 taxis (one will have an empty seat)
3 (a) Mon: £4.81 Tues: £9.46 Wed: £11.26 Thurs: £6.83 Fri: £15.67 Sat: £24.91
  (b) No

Unit A5/6 Problems involving division with remainders

1   Father Christmas wants to pack presents into boxes so that they fit into his sleigh better. He has to choose just one size of box so that he can stack them up.

If he has 120 presents to pack, how many boxes of each size would he *fill*?

(a)   Size A holds 3 toys ....   (b)   Size B holds 4 toys ....

(c)   Size C holds 5 toys ....   (d)   Size D holds 6 toys ....

(e)   Size E holds 7 toys ....   (f)   Size F holds 8 toys ....

(g)   Which box size would leave a toy left over? ....

2   A group of 53 Manchester United fans have come to Earth from a distant planet. They go in the club shop to buy souvenirs.

(a)   They have 3 identical feet each. How many football boots will 12 aliens need? ....

(b)   How many *pairs* of socks will 6 aliens need? ....

(c)   For dinner 9 aliens bought a box of 48 pies to share. How many of them would get an extra pie? ....

(d)   They each have three heads. They share a box of 100 cheap woolly hats from the market. How many aliens can wear one on each of their heads? ....

(e)   How many 6-seater taxis will they need for them all to get back to their spaceship? ....

3   The five staff at *Cut Backs Hair Stylists* share the tips they get each day. If they have a remainder they add it on to the next day's total.

Monday	£24.05
Tuesday	£47.32
Wednesday	£56.30
Thursday	£34.13
Friday	£78.39
Saturday	£124.51

(a)   How much did they each take home on:

Monday ....   Tuesday ....   Wednesday ....

Thursday ....   Friday ....   Saturday ....

(b)   Did they have a remainder at the end of the week? ....

Unit A5/7 Problems involving multiplication

PNS Framework objectives

- Solve one-step and two-step problems involving whole numbers and decimals and all four operations, choosing and using appropriate calculation strategies, including calculator use.
- Extend mental methods for whole-number calculations, for example to multiply a two-digit by a one-digit number (e.g. 12 × 9), to multiply by 25 (e.g. 16 × 25), to subtract one near-multiple of 1000 from another (e.g. 6070 − 4097).

Unit learning outcome

- To solve problems involving multiplication and halving.

Prior knowledge

- Able to halve three-digit and four-digit numbers.
- Able to multiply four-digit and five-digit numbers by a one-digit number.
- Able to multiply Tens and Units by Tens and Units.

Starter activity

- Brainstorm a list of classroom consumables on the whiteboard (e.g. types of exercise books, pens, glue pencils, felt pens, A4 paper, sticks, staples, etc.). By the side of each write how many of each item come in a pack. Estimate how many packs of each the class is likely to use in a term and in a whole school year.

Answers to A5/7

1   (a)   10 000 paper clips   (b)   960 books   (c)   600 pencils   (d)   375 books
     (e)   72 pairs of scissors   (f)   432 pens   (g)   30 000 staples   (h)   80 000 staples
     (i)   288 folders   (j)   75 000 sheets

2   (a)   87 books   (b)   116 books   (c)   90 English books, 120 Maths books

3   (a)   375 books   (b)   570 books   (c)   385 books   (d)   675 books

4   (a)   72 packs   (b)   96 rolls   (c)   114 sets of pens   (d)   51 sets of pens

Unit A5/7 Problems involving multiplication

Priory School is ordering stock for next year.

1   How many individual items will they get if they buy:

   (a)   8 boxes of 1250 paper clips? ....

   (b)   20 packs of 48 Maths exercise books? ....

   (c)   50 packs of 12 pencils? ....

   (d)   15 packs of 25 English exercise books? ....

   (e)   12 packs of 6 pairs of scissors? ....

   (f)   24 packs of 18 handwriting pens? ....

   (g)   6 boxes of 5000 size 10 staples? ....

   (h)   8 boxes of 10 000 size 26 staples? ....

   (i)   12 packs of 24 folders? ....

   (j)   150 reams of A4 paper? (a ream contains 500 sheets) ....

2   They expect each Year 5 child to use 3 English books and 4 Maths books in a year.

   (a)   How many English books will a class of 12 boys and 17 girls need? ....

   (b)   How many Maths books will the same Year 5 class need? ....

   (c)   The other Year 5 class has 16 boys and 14 girls. How many books do they need?
         .... English books and .... Maths books

3   Last year they ordered too many books so they are halving this year's order.

   (a)   Last year they bought 750 History books; this year they will buy ....

   (b)   Last year they bought 1140 Science books; this year they will buy ....

   (c)   Last year they bought 770 Geography books; this year they will buy ....

   (d)   Last year they bought 1350 word books; this year they will buy ....

4   Last year they ran out of some things. How many will they buy if:

   (a)   They double last year's order for 36 packs of pencil crayons? .... packs

   (b)   They double last year's order for 48 rolls of sticky tape? .... rolls

   (c)   They triple last year's order for 38 sets of thin coloured felt pens? .... sets

   (d)   They triple last year's order for 17 sets of thick coloured felt pens? .... sets

Unit A5/8 Problems involving halving

PNS Framework objectives

- Represent a puzzle or problem by identifying and recording the information or calculations needed to solve it; find possible solutions and confirm them in the context of the problem.
- Refine and use efficient written methods to multiply and divide HTU U, TU TU, U.t U and HTU U.
- Find fractions using division (e.g. $\frac{1}{100}$ of 5 kg), and percentages of numbers and quantities (e.g. 10%, 5% and 15% of £80).

Unit learning outcome

- To solve problems involving halving.

Prior knowledge

- Understands that halving is just another name for division by 2.
- Can quickly find halves of even integers.

Starter activities

- Challenge the children to work in pairs to see who can find a number that can be halved the most times without ending up with fractions. Stress that when they arrive at an odd number they have reached the end of their halving. Allow them time to try other starting numbers. Find out who claims to have the highest number of halvings and check that they are correct on the whiteboard. Suggest starting at 2000 – will this have a lot of halvings before arriving at an odd number? Try it out (four halvings). Now start at 1024 – will it have more or fewer halvings? Ask children to see which pair is the first to find out (10 halvings). Conclude that the size of the number is not the key to finding a number that can be halved so many times. Look at the next starter activity.
- Is there an easy way of finding a number that can be halved lots of times? What is the smallest odd number we could end up with? (1.) What number do we halve to get 1? (2.) What do we halve to get 2? (4.) We are just doubling.

EITHER ask children to key the following into a calculator 1 × 2 = then keep pressing = until the display can no longer display the answer.

OR do the following on a computer connected to your interactive whiteboard/data projector:

Open MS Excel, in cell A1 type 1, in cell A2 type =A1*2

Highlight cell A2, place cursor over the fill handle as illustrated and, while holding the left-hand mouse button, drag downwards. This will keep on doubling the previous number.

Hold down left mouse button on this corner and drag down

Answers to A5/8

1 (a) 1.92 m   (b) 0.24 m, or 24 cm

2 (a) 36 bulbs   (b) 54 bulbs   (c) 81 bulbs   (d) 81 is not divisible by 2, 81 is an odd number

3 (a) £96   (b) £48   (c) £24   (d) £12   (e) £6

Unit A5/8 Problems involving halving

1   Derek the gardener can only do things by halves. He was asked to trim a hedge which had grown to 3.84 metres high.

   (a)   He trimmed off half its height. How tall was it now? ....

   (b)   The customer asked him to do it again another three times. Each time Derek trimmed off half its height. How tall was it when he had finished? ....

2   Derek planted 24 tulip bulbs but the customer wanted more.

   (a)   He fetched half as many again and added them to the others he'd planted. How many were planted so far? ....

   (b)   The customer still wasn't happy, so Derek fetched more, half of the total already planted. How many had he planted now? ....

   (c)   Derek fetches even more bulbs, the same number as half the total planted so far. What is the total number of bulbs planted? ....

   (d)   Why couldn't Derek plant any more? ....

3   (a)   On Monday Derek worked for 8 hours at £12.00 per hour. How much did he earn? ....

   (b)   On Tuesday the customer wasn't happy and halved Derek's hourly rate of pay. How much did he earn in 8 hours on Tuesday? ....

   (c)   Wednesday was no better, the customer halved his rate of pay again! How much did he earn in 8 hours on Wednesday? ....

   (d)   Thursday, another day, another pay cut. How much for 8 hours' work on Thursday? ....

   (e)   On Friday Derek quit his job, after he received another halving of his pay. How much did he earn in 8 hours on Friday? ....

Unit A5/9 Problems with multiplication and division

PNS Framework objectives

- Plan and pursue an enquiry; present evidence by collecting, organising and interpreting information; suggest extensions to the enquiry.
- Use a calculator to solve problems, including those involving decimals or fractions (e.g. find $\frac{3}{4}$ of 150 g); interpret the display correctly in the context of measurement.

Unit learning outcome

- To solve problems with multiplication and division.

Prior knowledge

- Able to use long multiplication.
- Able to divide by a three-digit number.

Starter activity

- Look briefly at the scenario of the worksheet. Brainstorm what the group would like for a party. Consider savoury and sweet things to eat, plus sufficient drinks. What sort of quantities would be needed for the whole school? How many packs would be needed if items come in packs of 10, 12, 24, 48?

Answers to A5/9

1   (a) 2016 choc ices   (b) 864 plain biscuits   (c) 576 chocolate biscuits
    (d) 288 bags of crisps   (e) 2880 packs of chewing gum   (f) 1152 custard creams
    (g) 288 cartons of fruit juice   (h) 288 cans of pop   (i)   144 cheese straws

2   Each child will get:

3 plain biscuits	2 chocolate biscuits	4 custard creams
1 packet of crisps	$\frac{1}{2}$ a cheese straw	7 choc ices
1 carton of fruit juice	1 can of pop	10 packs of chewing gum

Unit A5/9 Problems with multiplication and division

Class 6 are planning the school's Christmas party.

They went to the warehouse to buy party food.

To save time they split up into three groups and met up at the checkout. Here is what each group bought:

Kerry's group

64 packets of 18 custard cream biscuits
16 packs of 18 cartons of fruit juice
30 packs of 12 choc ices
24 packets of 24 chocolate biscuits
2 boxes of 72 cheese straws

Jill's group

12 packs of 24 cans of pop
6 boxes of 48 packets of crisps
38 packs of 12 choc ices
27 packs of 32 plain biscuits

Darren's group

100 packs of 12 choc ices
80 boxes of 36 packs of chewing gum

---

1   What is the total number of:

    (a)   choc ices ....   (b)   plain biscuits ....

    (c)   chocolate biscuits ....   (d)   packets of crisps ....

    (e)   packs of chewing gum ....   (f)   custard cream biscuits ....

    (g)   cartons of fruit juice ....   (h)   cans of pop ....

    (i)   cheese straws ....

2   There were 288 children at the party. Everything is shared out equally – what will each child get?

plain biscuits ....   chocolate biscuits ....   custard creams ....

packets of crisps ....   cheese straws ....   choc ices ....

cartons of fruit juice ....   cans of pop ....   packs of chewing gum ......

Unit A5/10 Venn and Carroll diagrams

PNS Framework objectives

- Plan and pursue an enquiry; present evidence by collecting, organising and interpreting information; suggest extensions to the enquiry.
- Answer a set of related questions by collecting, selecting and organising relevant data; draw conclusions, using ICT to present features, and identify further questions to ask.

Unit learning outcome

- To solve problems involving Venn and Carroll diagrams.

Prior knowledge

- This unit reinforces Handling Data unit D5/3.
- Familiar with both types of diagram.

Starter activity

- Make a simple Venn diagram on the whiteboard with two criteria: 'I like football' and 'I like swimming'. Invite the children to write their names in the sector of the diagram which matches their preference.

  Draw a Carroll diagram grid with columns labelled 'I like football' and 'I don't like football', and rows labelled 'boys' and 'girls', or 'born Jan to June' and 'born July to Dec'. Point out that on the Carroll diagram they can only put their name in one column and one row. Those who like both must decide if football is their favourite.

Answers to A5/10

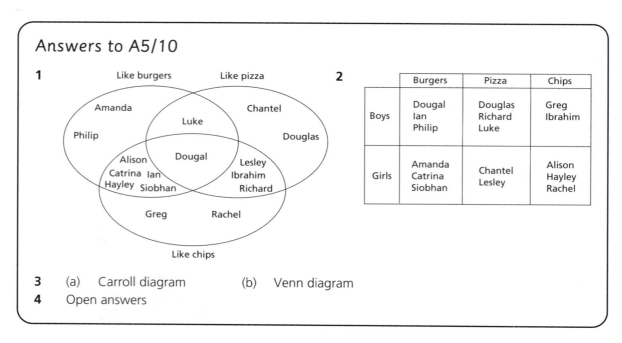

1

	Burgers	Pizza	Chips
Boys	Dougal Ian Philip	Douglas Richard Luke	Greg Ibrahim
Girls	Amanda Catrina Siobhan	Chantel Lesley	Alison Hayley Rachel

3 (a) Carroll diagram   (b) Venn diagram

4 Open answers

Unit A5/10 Venn and Carroll diagrams

Here are the results of a survey of which fast foods a group of children like.

☺ means 'favourite'
😐 means 'also like'

Girls	Fast foods we like		
	Burgers	Pizza	Chips
Amanda	☺		
Alison	😐		☺
Catrina	☺		😐
Chantel		☺	
Hayley	😐		☺
Lesley		☺	😐
Rachel			☺
Siobhan	☺		😐

Boys	Fast foods we like		
	Burgers	Pizza	Chips
Dougal	☺	😐	😐
Douglas		☺	
Greg			☺
Ian	☺		😐
Ibrahim		😐	☺
Luke	😐	☺	
Philip	☺		
Richard		☺	😐

1   Complete the *Venn* diagram to show who likes which fast food.

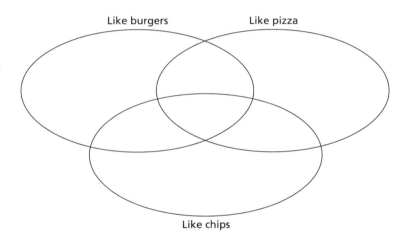

Like burgers   Like pizza

Like chips

2   Use this *Carroll* diagram to show the children's favourite fast foods.

	Burgers	Pizza	Chips
Boys			
Girls			

3   (a)   Which diagram separates boys from girls? ....
    (b)   Which diagram has more groups of children? ....

4   Write two questions about the data and give the correct answers.
    (a) .... answer ....
    (b) .... answer ....

Unit A5/11 Problems with area

PNS Framework objectives

- Solve one-step and two-step problems involving whole numbers and decimals and all four operations, choosing and using appropriate calculation strategies, including calculator use.
- Draw and measure lines to the nearest millimetre; measure and calculate the perimeter of regular and irregular polygons; use the formula for the area of a rectangle to calculate the rectangle's area.

Unit learning outcome

- To solve problems involving area including imperial units.

Prior knowledge

- This unit reinforces Measuring units M5/1, M5/3 and M5/4.
- Understands the term perimeter and knows it is measured in units of length.
- Understands the term area and knows it is two-dimensional and is measured in square units.

Starter activity

- Give children a long strip of card and ask them to put three folds in it to form a rectangle when the two ends are joined by a piece of sticky tape. Look at the accuracy of some: Are opposite sides equal? Are all four corners right angles?

  Give them a second strip of card, but this time instruct them to:

  Fold the strip exactly in half and cut it in two.

  Place one piece on top of the other and fold both in two to form a right angle.

  Separate the two pieces, flip one over and join them together with sticky tape to make a rectangle.

  Point out that for this second rectangle one length and width were made from one half of the original strip of card – so one length and one width equals half the perimeter of the rectangle.

Answers to A5/11

1. (a) and (b) Open answers, but one length plus one width of each of the four rectangles should add up to 24 m
   (c) $23 \, m \times 1 \, m = 23 \, m^2$ (d) $12 \, m \times 12 \, m = 144 \, m^2$ (e) $121 \, m^2$
2. (a) $600 \, m^2$ (b) $9 \, m \times 6 \, m$ (c) $54 \, m^2$ (d) $546 \, m^2$ too little
3. Nursery: $300 \, m^2$ Reception: $160 \, m^2$ Class 1: $160 \, m^2$ Class 2: $150 \, m^2$
   Total: $770 \, m^2$

Unit A5/11 Problems with area

1   The head has decided to fence off an area of the field to stop the nursery children
    wandering off. He has 48 m of wire mesh.

(a)   Draw four ways he could make a rectangular
      pen with a perimeter of 48 m.

Use 1 square to represent 1 metre.

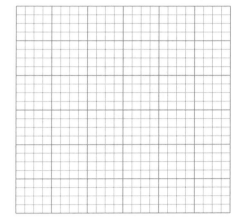

(b)   Label the length, width and area of each of
      your designs.

(c)   Using whole metres, what size of pen would
      have the smallest area? ....

(d)   What size of pen would have the largest
      area? ....

(e)   What is the difference in area between the
      largest and the smallest? ....

2   The headteacher decided to have a playground covered with rubber safety matting. He
    measured 30 m × 20 m, but on the telephone ordered 30 feet by 20 feet by mistake.

(a)   Work out the area of matting he wanted in m² ....

(b)   Use a calculator to change 30 feet by 20 feet into metric measurements ....
      m × .... m

1 foot = approximately 0.3 metres.

(c)   How many m² of matting did he order by mistake? ....

(d)   How much too little or too much did he order? ....

3   Some of the classrooms need new carpet. Work out the area of carpet needed, then add
    up the total area.

Classroom	length	width	area
Nursery	25 m	12 m	.... m²
Reception	20 m	8 m	.... m²
Class 1	16 m	10 m	.... m²
Class 2	15 m	10 m	.... m²
		Total area of carpet needed	.... m²

Unit A5/12 Problems involving time intervals

PNS Framework objectives

- Represent a puzzle or problem by identifying and recording the information or calculations needed to solve it; find possible solutions and confirm them in the context of the problem.
- Read timetables and time using 24-hour clock notation; use a calendar to calculate time intervals.

Unit learning outcome

- To solve problems involving time intervals.

Prior knowledge

- This unit reinforces Measuring units M5/5 and M5/6.
- Familiar with the 24-hour clock.
- Able to work out time intervals (as per M5/6).
- Able to total periods of time.

Starter activity

- On the whiteboard write down how *you* might spend a typical school day. Demonstrate the following methods of finding how long you spend doing each activity.

  Use the counting-on method:

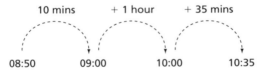

1 hour + 35 mins + 10 mins = **1 hour 45 mins**

  or the subtraction method of finding time intervals by subtraction, e.g.

1 Exchange 1 hour for 60 minutes

2 Subtract 50 from the 60 minutes then add on the 35 minutes

  Add together the times you spend 'teaching', dividing the minutes by 60 when necessary to exchange for hours.

Answers to A5/12

1 (a) 5 hours 19 minutes (b) 5 hours 45 minutes (c) 1 hour 20 minutes
 (d) 7 minutes (e) 5 minutes
2 Open answers

Unit A5/12 Problems involving time intervals

This is how Mika the cat spent part of a day:

At 07:30 he came in after a night outside in the rain.

From 07:30 till 07:35 he dried himself by lying on Alison's new quilt cover.

From 07:35 till 08:10 he miaowed and looked for someone to feed him.

From 08:10 till 08:13 he ate his first meal.

From 08:14 till 11:50 he slept on top of the ironing.

From 11:51 till 12:07 he asked to be fed again.

From 12:08 till 12:10 he ate his second meal.

From 12:11 till 17:30 he was outside 'hunting'.

From 17:31 till 19:40 he slept on top of the central heating boiler.

From 19:41 till 20:10 he asked to be fed again!

From 20:11 till 20:13 he ate another meal.

1　Find out how long he spent:

　　(a)　hunting ....　　(b)　sleeping ....　　(c)　asking for food ....

　　(d)　eating ....　　(e)　lying on a bed ....

2　(a)　Use this chart to record how you spend a school day

From	Until		Length of time

　　(b)　How much time do you spend in school? ....

　　(c)　How long do you spend working? ....

　　(d)　How long do you spend playing? ....

Unit A5/13 Problems with angles, shape and co-ordinates

PNS Framework objectives

- Explore patterns, properties and relationships and propose a general statement involving numbers or shapes; identify examples for which the statement is true or false.
- Estimate, draw and measure acute and obtuse angles using an angle measurer or protractor to a suitable degree of accuracy; calculate angles in a straight line.

Unit learning outcome

- To solve problems involving angles, shape and co-ordinates.

Prior knowledge

- This unit relates to work covered on understanding shape units S5/1, S5/2, S5/3, S5/6 and S5/7.
- Able to draw angles with a protractor.
- Knowledge of line symmetry, co-ordinates and 2-D and 3-D shapes.

Starter activities

- Use a set of cards with 2-D shapes on to play 'snap'.
- Cut a square in two diagonally to produce two right-angled isosceles triangles. Cut one of these in half, bisecting the right angle to make two smaller right-angled isosceles triangles. Continue to bisect one of each pair of triangles until they become too small to continue. Challenge children to reassemble the original square.
- Play 'Find the treasure': one player marks where his treasure is buried on an unseen grid while the other players guess where it is by nominating co-ordinates. The first player gives a clue by telling the others how many grid squares their guess was from the treasure. Using a duplicate copy of the grid the other players refine their guess. Play continues until they name the co-ordinates of the treasure.

Answers to A5/13

1 To check this question it might be easier to make card templates of the parallelograms which can be placed over the child's drawing to check. It may be necessary to flip and rotate the template depending on which of the two lengths of side they started with.
   (a) Drawing of a parallelogram with sides of 4 cm and 5 cm, and angles of 40° and 140°
   (b) Drawing of a parallelogram with sides of 6 cm and 3 cm, and angles of 80° and 100°

2 and 3 Pupils' answers will vary

Unit A5/13 Problems with angles, shape and co-ordinates

1   Draw parallelograms which have:

   (a)   2 angles of 40°, 2 sides of 5 cm and 2 sides of 4 cm.

   (b)   2 angles of 80°, 2 sides of 6 cm and 2 sides of 3 cm.

2   Draw shapes that match these descriptions:

   (a)   a symmetrical triangle with one right angle.

   (b)   a symmetrical pentagon with three right angles.

   (c)   a pentagon with every line and angle different.

   (d)   a triangular prism with right-angled triangular faces at each end.

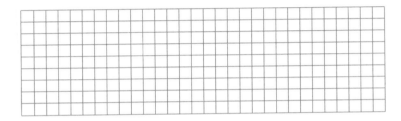

3   (a)   Using the lines of this grid, make a simple picture or design.

   (b)   Use co-ordinates to write instructions for a partner who has not seen your design.

   (c)   Swap instructions with a partner; each of you try to draw the other's design on squared paper just from the written instructions.

   (d)   Check to see if both versions of each design look the same.

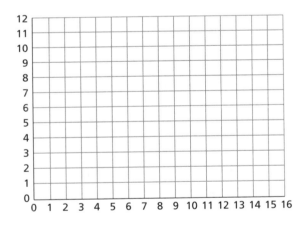

Unit A6/1 Problems involving adding 0.1 and 0.01, and forwards and back

PNS Framework objectives

- Solve multi-step problems, and problems involving fractions, decimals and percentages; choose and use appropriate calculation strategies at each stage, including calculator use.
- Calculate mentally with integers and decimals: U.t U.t, TU U, TU U, U.t U, U.t U.

Unit learning outcome

- Problems involving adding 0.1 and 0.01, and forwards and back.

Prior knowledge

- Competent with addition involving TU.t and TU.th.
- Able to round to the nearest whole litre.

Starter activity

- Make a decimal converter (as illustrated). Use it on the whiteboard to solve two-stage problems such as increasing or decreasing an integer by one-tenth or one-hundredth.

  First find the tenth or hundredth then write it beneath the integer (with decimal point), then add or subtract as appropriate.

  Point out that in reality it is the numerals that are moving columns, the column labels are being moved to avoid having to unscrew the whiteboard from the wall!

Place the decimal converter over a 2-digit integer

H	T	U	$\frac{1}{10}$	$\frac{1}{100}$
	4	2 $\cdot$		

Slide it one column to the left to find one-tenth

H	T	U	$\frac{1}{10}$	$\frac{1}{100}$
		4 $\cdot$	2	

Answers to A6/1

1 (a) 27.9 l   (b) 54.4 l   (c) 42.43 l   (d) 38.5 l   (e) 34.41 l   (f) 45.01 l
(g) 28 + 55 + 43 + 39 + 34 + 46 = 246 litres altogether
(h) 28 + 54 + 42 + 39 + 34 + 46 = 243 litres altogether
(i) The manager charged for approximately 3 more litres than he actually sold

2 (a) £25.25   (b) £32.32   (c) £28.28   (d) £43.43   (e) £19.19   (f) £52.52
(g) These customers were overcharged £1.99 altogether

3 (a) £18   (b) £16.20   (c) £40.50   (d) £28.80   (e) £9.90   (f) £0.54
(g) £12.66

Unit A6/1 Problems involving adding 0.1 and 0.01, and forwards and back

1   The dishonest manager of a petrol station has altered the settings on the petrol pumps.
     Every time a customer has finished filling up it adds 0.1 of a litre on to the meter reading.
     Here are the meter readings for six customers. Write in how much fuel they really had.

   (a) 28 litres ....   (b) 54.5 litres ....   (c) 42.53 litres ....

   (d) 38.6 litres ....   (e) 34.51 litres ....   (f) 46.11 litres ....

   (g) Round the meter readings to the nearest whole litre then total them up.

        28 litres + ... + ... + ... + ... + ... = ... litres altogether.

   (h) Round the *actual* amounts of fuel sold (your answers to question 1) to the nearest
        whole litre then total them up.

        28 litres + ... + ... + ... + ... + ... = ... litres altogether.

   (i) Use your totals from (g) and (h) to find the approximate difference between the fuel
        bought and the amount of fuel charged for: ....

2   He also overcharges customers using the cash register. It automatically increases each bill
     by one-hundredth (1%). It does this by multiplying the correct amount by 0.01 and
     adding it on to the bill.
     What will these bills be increased to?

   (a) £25 £ ....   (b) £32 £ ....   (c) £28 £ ....

   (d) £43 £ ....   (e) £19 £ ....   (f) £52 £ ....

   (g) How much did he overcharge these six customers altogether? £ ....

3   When his crime is discovered the owner decides to give all customers a 10% discount to
     regain their trust. To do this the cash register multiplies the amount by 0.1 and subtracts
     it from the bill.
     What will these bills be reduced to?

   (a) £20 £ ....   (b) £18 £ ....   (c) £45 £ ....

   (d) £32 £ ....   (e) £11 £ ....   (f) £0.60 £ ....

   (g) How much did these six customers save altogether? £ ....

Unit A6/2 Problems involving multiples, prime numbers and hexagonal numbers

PNS Framework objective

- Represent and interpret sequences, patterns and relationships involving numbers and shapes; suggest and test hypotheses; construct and use simple expressions and formulae in words then symbols (e.g. the cost of c pens at 15 pence each is 15c pence).

Unit learning outcome

- To solve problems involving multiples, prime numbers and hexagonal numbers.

Prior knowledge

- Knows what a prime number is.
- Understands the term 'multiple' and knows multiples of 2, 3, 4 and 5 to at least 36.

Starter activities

- Tessellate hexagon templates. (Tip: draw around a hexagon template and staple two or three sheets of paper beneath so that you can cut out three or four at a time.)
- Play 'Multiple or prime': Divide the group into two teams. Shuffle a set of number cards and show them one at a time. As each card is shown, children from both teams can call out 'multiple' or 'prime'. Take the answer of the first to call – if they are correct give their team 2 points, if wrong give the other team 1 point. Use tallying to keep the score and play until one team has 20 points.

Answers to A6/2

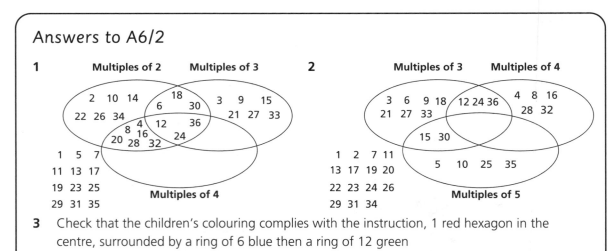

1

Multiples of 2   Multiples of 3

2 10 14   18
22 26 34   6   30   3 9 15
        8 4 12   36   21 27 33
      20 16 32   24
        28

1 5 7
11 13 17
19 23 25   **Multiples of 4**
29 31 35

2

Multiples of 3   Multiples of 4

3 6 9 18 12 24 36   4 8 16
21 27 33   28 32

        15 30

1 2 7 11
13 17 19 20   5   10 25 35
22 23 24 26   **Multiples of 5**
29 31 34

3 Check that the children's colouring complies with the instruction, 1 red hexagon in the centre, surrounded by a ring of 6 blue then a ring of 12 green

4 $19 + (3 \times 6) = $ **37**, $37 + (4 \times 6) = $ **61**, $61 + (5 \times 6) = $ **91**

Unit A6/2 Problems involving multiples, prime numbers and hexagonal numbers

1   Place the numbers 1 to 36 on this Venn diagram.

2   Now place the same numbers on this Venn diagram.

Hint: most prime numbers belong outside the rings.

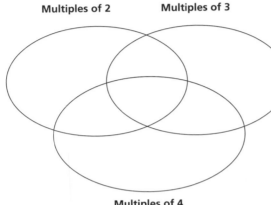

Multiples of 2   Multiples of 3

Multiples of 4

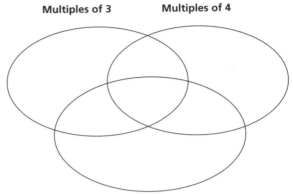

Multiples of 3   Multiples of 4

Multiples of 5

3   (a)   Find the middle hexagon and colour it red.

   (b)   Surround the red hexagon with a ring of blue hexagons.

   (c)   Colour the remaining hexagons green.

   (d)   Complete the following:

         .... red + ... blue = ...

         .... red + ... blue + ...

         green = ...

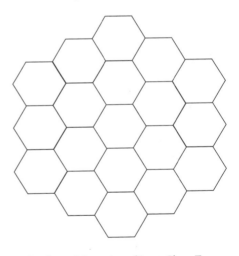

You have been drawing hexagonal numbers.

You started with 1 and added 1 multiple of 6 (coloured blue) making $1 + (1 \times 6) = 7$.

For the second hexagonal number you began with 7 and added 2 multiples of six:

$7 + (2 \times 6) = 19$.

To find the next hexagonal number, start with the last one and add one more multiple of 6 than last time.

4   What are the next three hexagonal numbers?

$19 + (3 \times 6) = ...,$ .... $+ (4 \times 6) = ...,$ .... $+ (.......... \times 6) = ...$

If you have time, use a hexagon template and a large sheet of paper to see if you are right.

Unit A6/3 Calculator problems involving volume, mass, ratio and fraction of an amount

PNS Framework objectives

- Solve multi-step problems, and problems involving fractions, decimals and percentages; choose and use appropriate calculation strategies at each stage, including calculator use.
- Select and use standard metric units of measure and convert between units using decimals to two places (e.g. change 2.75 l to 2750 ml, or vice versa).

Unit learning outcome

- To solve calculator problems involving volume, mass, ratio and fraction of an amount.

Prior knowledge

- Familiar with metric units for length, mass and volume.
- Competent with a calculator.

Starter activity

- Use an electronic balance to weigh a litre of water. To do this you need a measured litre in an easy-to-pour container and an empty container to place on the balance prior to resetting the display to zero. Now measure the volume of 1 kg of water by weighing the water till it is exactly 1 kg (a syringe is a useful tool for fine adjustments), then carefully transfer to a measuring container.

  Try repeating the same with smaller amounts of water.

Answers to A6/3

1 (a) 280 plain, 40 patterned   (b) 532 plain, 76 patterned   (c) 1344 plain, 192 patterned
   (d) 4900 plain, 700 patterned   (e) $\frac{7}{8}$ plain   (f) $\frac{1}{8}$ patterned

2 (a) 240 m³   (b) 240 000 litres

3 (a) 9000 ml   (b) 9 l   (c) 244 009 l

4 (a) 240 000 kg   (b) 240 tonnes

Unit A6/3 Calculator problems involving volume, mass, ratio and fraction of an amount

It would be a good idea to use a calculator for questions 2 to 5.

1   Priory School is having a swimming pool built. Most of the pool will be in plain blue tiles but two in every 16 will be patterned.

How many plain and patterned tiles will there be when the tiler has stuck on:

(a)   320 tiles: .... plain and .... patterned

(b)   608 tiles: .... plain and .... patterned

(c)   1536 tiles: .... plain and .... patterned

(d)   5600 tiles: .... plain and .... patterned

What fraction (in its *simplest form*) of the tiles are:

(e)   patterned? ....

(f)   plain? ....

2   The caretaker needs to measure how much water it holds so that he can put in the correct amount of chemicals.

To help him the headteacher wrote a formula on the back of an old envelope. The caretaker wrote the measurements underneath.

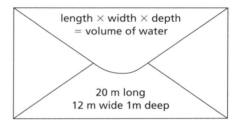

length × width × depth
= volume of water

20 m long
12 m wide 1m deep

(a)   What is the volume of water in cubic metres? ....

(b)   Use this formula $l = m^3 \times 1000$ to change it into litres: ....

3   The chemicals have to be added in the ratio of 3 ml to every 80 l.

(a)   How many millilitres of chemical are added? ....

(b)   How many litres of chemical are added? ....

(c)   What is the total volume of pool water (water + chemicals)? ....

4   One litre of pure water weighs 1 kg. If the water from the tap is pure, what did it weigh:

(a)   in kg? ....   (b)   in tonnes (1 tonne = 1000 kg)? ....

Unit A6/4 Problems involving addition, subtraction, doubling and halving

PNS Framework objectives

- Solve multi-step problems, and problems involving fractions, decimals and percentages; choose and use appropriate calculation strategies at each stage, including calculator use.
- Use a calculator to solve problems involving multi-step calculations.

Unit learning outcome

- To solve problems involving addition, subtraction, doubling and halving.

Prior knowledge

- Able to use a calculator accurately.

Starter activity

- Use the sports page of a newspaper listing football results and the 'gate' or 'attendance figures' for different matches. Alternatively download results from the Internet either using a search engine to find media reviews of matches, or go directly to the Football Association website (www.thefa.com) to find results – attendance figures are included in the match 'stats'. Look at the size of the numbers. Remind children of the convention of leaving a grouping of integer numerals in threes (from the right) if the number has five digits or more. Point out that the old system of using commas every three integer digits is falling out of use. The old system sometimes caused confusion since some countries such as France still use a comma instead of a decimal point.

Answers to A6/4

1	(a)	10	(b)	11	(c)	522	
2	(a)	16248	(b)	10832			
3	(a)	13004	(b)	8	(c)	8672	(d) 4340
4	(a)	4062	(b)	5416	(c)	8124	(d) 6502
5	(a)	29252	(b)	14626			

Unit A6/4 Problems involving addition, subtraction, doubling and halving

1   Here are the scores of a cricket match, just before the winning team began its second innings.

Yorkshire	1st innings	130	runs
Lancashire	1st innings	251	runs
Yorkshire	2nd innings	130	runs
Lancashire	2nd innings	....	runs

A6/4

  (a)   How many runs do Lancashire need to win by 1 run? ....

  (b)   They win by 2 runs. Complete the results table.

  (c)   What is the total number of runs scored? ....

2   On day 1 of the match, 8124 spectators had arrived by 12:00. The crowd had doubled by mid-afternoon.

  (a)   How many spectators were there by mid-afternoon? ....

  (b)   By close of play one-third of the spectators had already left; how many remained till the end? ....

3   By 12:00 on day 2 there were 6506 Lancashire fans and 6498 Yorkshire fans.

  (a)   How many fans were there altogether? ....

  (b)   How many more Lancashire fans were there? ....

  (c)   During the afternoon $\frac{2}{3}$ of the Yorkshire fans went home. How many spectators were left? ....

  (d)   How many more Lancashire fans than Yorkshire fans were there by the end of the afternoon? ....

4   Half of the spectators on each day were retired people. How many attended:

  (a)   in the morning on the first day? ....

  (b)   in the evening of the first day? ....

  (c)   in the afternoon of the first day? ....

  (d)   in the morning on the second day? ....

5   All the spectators were counted as they came through the gate on each day.

  (a)   What was the gate total for both days? ....

  (b)   What was the gate number for retired people? ....

Unit A6/5 Problems using rounding to make estimates prior to calculations

PNS Framework objectives

- Suggest, plan and develop lines of enquiry; collect, organise and represent information, interpret results and review methods; identify and answer related questions.
- Use a calculator to solve problems involving multi-step calculations.

Unit learning outcome

- To solve problems using rounding to make estimates prior to making accurate calculations.

Prior knowledge

- Able to round numbers to the nearest 5, 10, 100, 1000, etc.

Starter activities

- Discuss how estimated figures are often more useful than actual figures, especially when actual figures change all the time, e.g. population. Use rounded figures to estimate how many children there are in the school then compare with actual figures. Brainstorm what would be the best number to round to estimate: football crowds, books on the shelves, population.
- Use the Internet to find population data and round it to easy-to-handle numbers.
- Round the population data opposite – discuss what would be the best unit to round to.

	Population (2001 Census)
London	7 172 091
Birmingham	970 892
Leeds	715 404
Glasgow	577 869
Edinburgh	448 624
Manchester	392 819
Cardiff	305 353
Belfast	276 459
Wolverhampton	236 582

Answers to A6/5

1   Answers will vary according to what they round the numbers to

2

	Paper clips	Staples approx.	Felt pens Thick	Thin	Ballpoint pens Red	Black	Green	Rolls of sticky tape	Glue sticks
Estimate	Answers will vary according to rounding method used.								
Actual	8748	319 500	137	1131	61	36	96	25½	37
Difference	Answers will vary according to rounding method used.								

3   Answers will vary according to what they round the numbers to

Unit A6/5 Problems using rounding to make estimates prior to calculations

Some teachers at Priory School have complained about not having enough equipment. The head has rummaged through their desks to see who has what.

	Paper clips	Staples approx.	Felt pens Thick	Thin	Ballpoint pens Red	Black	Green	Rolls of sticky tape	Glue sticks
Nursery	5354	10 300	24	365	24	6	12	5 rolls	8
Reception	2268	5400	47	425	5	7	12	3½ rolls	6
Class 1	268	27 900	25	150	8	6	12	4 rolls	3
Class 2	654	160 000	12	75	10	4	12	8 rolls	7
Class 3	165	48 600	8	36	7	5	12	3½ rolls	4
Class 4	3	150	4	17	0	1	12	none	1
Class 5	17	62 200	7	28	3	2	12	½ a roll	5
Class 6	19	4950	10	35	4	3	12	1 roll	3

1   Round the figures to simpler numbers and write them in the table below.

	Paper clips	Staples approx.	Felt pens Thick	Thin	Ballpoint pens Red	Black	Green	Rolls of sticky tape	Glue sticks
Nursery									
Reception									
Class 1									
Class 2									
Class 3									
Class 4									
Class 5									
Class 6									

2   (a)   Add the rounded numbers using pencil and paper and put your answers in the *Estimate* row below.

	Paper clips	Staples approx.	Felt pens Thick	Thin	Ballpoint pens Red	Black	Green	Rolls of sticky tape	Glue sticks
Estimate									
Actual									
Difference ±									

(b)   Use a calculator to find the *actual* totals (*hint: do each total twice to make sure you are right*).

(c)   Find the difference between your estimates and the actual totals. Don't forget to use a + or – sign.

3   Use the estimated totals to find out *approximately* what each class would have if the head shared everything out equally among all the classes.

Paper clips	Staples approx.	Felt pens Thick	Thin	Ballpoint pens Red	Black	Green	Rolls of sticky tape	Glue sticks

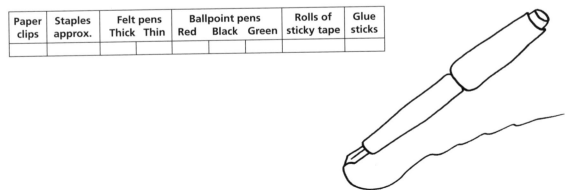

Unit A6/6 Calculator problems involving cost, budgeting and rounding

PNS Framework objectives

- Tabulate systematically the information in a problem or puzzle; identify and record the steps or calculations needed to solve it, using symbols where appropriate; interpret solutions in the original context and check their accuracy.
- Use a calculator to solve problems involving multi-step calculations.

Unit learning outcome

- To solve calculator problems involving cost, budgeting and rounding to the nearest 0.1.

Prior knowledge

- Firm understanding of place value including decimals.
- Able to use a calculator and round the result to the nearest tenth.

Starter activity

- Play 'Calculator race': Divide into two teams, each child (or pair) equipped with a calculator. Start by asking them to do a simple calculation. Take the answer of the first to call – if they are correct give their team 2 points, if wrong give the other team 1 point. After a few goes tell them that from now on all the questions will be division. Begin using multiples of the divisor. After a few more announce that some answers are going to involve decimals but you only want answers to one decimal place (demonstrate if necessary). Now use questions using non-multiples of the divisor (e.g. 47 ÷ 6).

Answers to A6/6

1 (a) 160 for £2.45   (b) 2 kg for £3.74   (c) 8 for £1.50
   (d) 12 for £1.80   (e) 4 for £1.56   (f) 3 litres for £1.65

2 (a) and (b) Children's answers will vary; but there must be change from the £16 budget

3 (a) 1.9p   (b) 1.8p   (c) 17.4p   (d) 15p
   (e) 16.7p   (f) 33p   (g) 29.4p   (h) 24.9p

Unit A6/6 Calculator problems involving cost, budgeting and rounding

1 Colin is doing his weekly shopping. He often buys the 'best bargain'. Find the best bargains for him from these choices and draw a circle around it.

   (a) tea bags: 40 for 75p, 80 for £1.45, 160 for £2.45, trial pack of 16 for 49p

   (b) oven chips: £1.33 for 500 g, £1.63 for 750 g, £3.00 for 1.5 kg, £3.74 for 2 kg

   (c) oranges: 3 for 81p, 5 for £1.24, 8 for £1.50, 10 for £2.13

   (d) fish fingers: 10 for £1.74, 12 for £1.80, 18 for £3.00

   (e) toilet rolls: 2 for 81p, 4 for £1.56, 8 for £3.38, 12 for £4.88

   (f) pop: 42p for 0.33 l can, 63p for ½ l bottle, £1.25 for 2 l bottle, £1.65 for 3 l bottle

2 Colin has £16 to spend.

   (a) Decide what he should buy and add up his bill.

   (b) How much change would he have? ....

		Price
......	tea bags	....
......	g of oven chips	....
......	oranges	....
......	fish fingers	....
......	toilet rolls	....
....	of lemonade	....
	Total cost	....

3 Work out the cost of each of the following items. You will have to round some to the nearest tenth of a penny.

   (a) 1 tea bag at 75p for 40 ....   (b) 1 tea bag at £1.45 for 80 ....

   (c) 1 fish finger at 10 for £1.74 .... (d) 1 fish finger at 12 for £1.80 ....

   (e) 1 fish finger at 18 for £3.00 .... (f) 1 orange at 3 for 99p ....

   (g) 1 orange at 5 for £1.47 ....   (h) 1 orange at 8 for £1.99 ....

Unit A6/7 Problems involving multiple doubling and trebling

PNS Framework objectives

- Tabulate systematically the information in a problem or puzzle; identify and record the steps or calculations needed to solve it, using symbols where appropriate; interpret solutions in the original context and check their accuracy.
- Use a calculator to solve problems involving multi-step calculations.

Unit learning outcome

- To solve problems involving multiple doubling and trebling.

Prior knowledge

- Able to use a calculator accurately.

Starter activity

- Show the children how to use the constant function on their calculators, usually achieved by keying in a number, the operation symbol then the equals sign, for example:

  [5] [+] [=] [=] [=] will give you 10, 15, 20, etc.

  [5] [×] [=] [=] [=] will give you 25, 125, 625, etc.

  Ask the children to key in a number and operation symbol and count how many presses of the equals key it takes before the display runs out of space. Use an addition constant to quickly find multiples of a number, e.g. to find 20 × 6 key in 6 × and press the equals key 20 times. Try multiples of larger numbers.

Answers to A6/7

1	Marluk Bank	Pingasut Bank
	(a) 40 Gluggs	135 Gluggs
	(b) 160 Gluggs	1215 Gluggs
	(c) 1280 Gluggs	32 805 Gluggs
	(d) 5120 Gluggs	295 245 Gluggs

2 6 weeks

3 (a) 21 weeks   (b) 13 weeks

Unit A6/7 Problems involving multiple doubling and trebling

You will need a calculator for this unit.

There are 2 banks on the planet *Smethom Nova*. The currency is the *Glugg*.

The *Marluk Bank* will double your money every week.

The *Pingasut Bank* will treble your money every week.

1   If you invested 5 Gluggs, how much would it be worth after:

		In the *Marluk* Bank	In the *Pingasut* Bank
(a)	3 weeks	....	....
(b)	5 weeks	....	....
(c)	8 weeks	....	....
(d)	10 weeks	....	....

> You can use this space to help work out your answers

2   Lorac invests 10 Gluggs in the Marluk Bank.
On the same day Yelsel invests a modest Glugg in the Pingasut Bank.
How many weeks will it be before Yelsel has more Gluggs in the bank than Lorac? ....

3   Nala is saving up for a holiday to Earth.
He needs 1 million Gluggs to go self-catering, and another $\frac{1}{2}$ million Gluggs for food and spending money. At the moment he only has 1 Glugg to invest.

(a)   How long will it take to have enough for his holiday if he puts it in the Marluk Bank?

    ....

(b)   How long will it take to have enough for his holiday if he puts it in the Pingasut Bank?

    ....

Interesting fact: 'Marluk' and 'Pingasut' are the Inuit words for 2 and 3!

Unit A6/8 Problems involving multiple doubling and halving (with remainders)

PNS Framework objective

- Solve multi-step problems, and problems involving fractions, decimals and percentages; choose and use appropriate calculation strategies at each stage, including calculator use.

Unit learning outcome

- To solve problems involving multiple doubling and halving (with remainders).

Prior knowledge

- Able to quickly find doubles and halves of two- and three-digit numbers.

Starter activity

- 'Halving countdowns': Set the children the challenge of finding a number less than 1000 which can be repeatedly halved a number of times before arriving at an odd number – who can find a number with the most halving steps? Change the rules to allow them to add or subtract 1 when they arrive at an odd number and see who has a starter number with the greatest number of halvings. Discuss if there is an easy way of choosing the optimum number to start with – begin with 1 and keep doubling up until you reach 512 (the next doubling takes you over 1000).

Answers to A6/8

1	(a) 9 weeks	(b)	4 pet lambs
2	(a) 9 weeks	(b)	No pet lambs
3	(a) 10 weeks	(b)	4 turkeys
4	(a) 96 bags	(b)	189 bags altogether

Unit A6/8 Problems involving multiple doubling and halving (with remainders)

Try to work these out in your head. You may need to use pencil and paper to help.

1   Every spring a farmer decides to send half of his lambs to market every week. Each time he has an odd number, he gives a lamb to his daughter to keep as a pet. Last year he began with 600 lambs.
   (a)   How many weeks did it take to get them to market? ....
   (b)   How many pet lambs did his daughter get? ....

2   This year he had 512 lambs ready to go to market.
   (a)   How many weeks did it take to get them to market this year? ....
   (b)   How many pet lambs did his daughter get this year? ....

3   In the autumn each week he sells half his sacks of potatoes to a supermarket. This year he started with 1200 sacks. When he has an odd number of sacks he swaps one sack for a turkey.
   (a)   How many weeks did he send potatoes to market? ....
   (b)   How many turkeys did he end up with? ....

4   In the first week that he harvested his beans he sent 3 bags to market. Each week he doubled the number of bags he sent.
   (a)   How many bags of beans did he send to market in the sixth week? ....
   (b)   How many bags of beans did he send in the first 6 weeks? ....

Unit A6/9 Problems with squaring and division

PNS Framework objectives

- Tabulate systematically the information in a problem or puzzle; identify and record the steps or calculations needed to solve it, using symbols where appropriate; interpret solutions in the original context and check their accuracy.
- Use knowledge of multiplication facts to derive quickly squares of numbers to 12 × 12 and the corresponding squares of multiples of 10.

Unit learning outcome

- To solve problems with squaring and division.

Prior knowledge

- Able to break problems down into a sequence of operations.

Starter activity

- Ask everyone to think of a number less than 10 but keep it secret. Ask them to square it, then double the result, then divide by the number they started with. Ask a few people in turn what number they finished with and tell them the number they started with – half of the number they finished with. Explain how this 'trick' works – the doubling and your halving cancel each other out, and the multiplication and division by the original number also cancel each other out. Invite them to make up their own 'trick'.

Answers to A6/9

1 (a) 50 625 g/50.625 kg	(b) Wednesday	(c) 2025 g/2.025 kg each
2 (a) 625 pizzas	(b) 6561 pies	(c) £65 536
3 Nothing! 1 × 1 = 1		
4 25 pizzas each		
5 729 spectators		
6 An average of £1024 per day		

Unit A6/9 Problems with squaring and division

A mad scientist has invented a machine that copies anything. Every day anything left within range of the scanner will multiply by itself. If you put 100 g of chips by it, on Sunday there would be 1 kg (10 000 g) of chips by Monday!

1   On Monday his wife placed 15 g of chocolate by it.

    (a)   How much chocolate was there by Wednesday? ....

    (b)   She removed it from the machine when the weight of the chocolate exceeded 50 kg. What day was this? ....

    (c)   She managed to get rid of the chocolate, with the help of the other 24 members of her slimming club. How much did they each have to eat? ....

2   While his wife was feeling ill, the scientist did some experiments. What did he have when:

    (a)   he left 5 pizzas in for two days? ....

    (b)   he left 3 pies in for three days? ....

    (c)   he left £2 in for four days? ....

3   What happened when the cat went to sleep under the scanner and was accidentally locked in for a week? ....

4   When the slimming club recovered from the chocolate they shared out the pizzas. How many did they have each? ....

5   To get rid of the pies he stood outside a football ground and gave 9 pies to every spectator. How many spectators were there? ....

6   He managed to spend all the money in just 64 days. *On average*, how much did he spend each day? ....

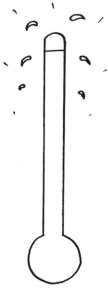

Unit A6/10 Problems involving handling data

PNS Framework objectives

- Tabulate systematically the information in a problem or puzzle; identify and record the steps or calculations needed to solve it, using symbols where appropriate; interpret solutions in the original context and check their accuracy.
- Describe and interpret results and solutions to problems using the mode, range, median and mean.

Unit learning outcome

- To solve problems involving handling data.

Prior knowledge

- This unit relates to work covered in Handling Data units D6/1 to D6/5.
- Familiar with the terms 'mean', 'mode', 'median' and 'range' and how they are derived.

Starter activity

- 'Data quiz': Divide the group into teams. For each question write a set of numbers on the whiteboard and declare that you want either the mean, mode, median or range. Identify the first two or three hands to go up and ask the first for their answer. If correct award two points, if wrong deduct a point from their team and ask the second person to raise their hand. Take the answer from the first hand to go up. Use both odd and even sets of data, particularly when looking for the median – explain the trick of adding the two middle numbers and halving the total when finding the median of an even number of data.

Answers to A6/10

1

	Mean	Mode	Median	Range
Year 3	7	8	8	8
Year 4	8	6	7	7
Year 5	11.7	14	12.5	13
Year 6	13	5	11	21

2 (a) Shade: Mon (8), Thurs (8), Mon (8), Wed (9), Thurs (11) and Fri (8)

   (b) Shade: Tues (6), Fri (6), Tues (5), Wed (5) and Fri (6)

   (c) Shade: Tues (5), Thurs (7), Fri (13), Tues (12), Thurs (11) and Fri (8)

3 (a) 8   (b) 5   (c) 4

Unit A6/10 Problems involving handling data

Here are the house points totals for two weeks.

	Week 1					Week 2				
	Mon	Tues	Wed	Thurs	Fri	Mon	Tues	Wed	Thurs	Fri
Year 3	9	5	5	8	3	8	4	9	11	8
Year 4	11	6	11	8	6	12	5	5	10	6
Year 5	14	5	15	7	13	18	12	12	11	8
Year 6	18	12	5	9	26	22	7	7	16	10

1   For each year group work out its two-week mean, mode, median and range.

	Mean	Mode	Median	Range
Year 3				
Year 4				
Year 5				
Year 6				

Reminder:

Mean: the total divided by how many numbers you added.

Mode: the commonest number.

Median: the middle value when they are put in order; *but* if there is an even number of values like here the median is between the two middle values. (*Hint: if the two middle numbers are different, add them together and halve the answer*.)

Range: the difference between the highest and lowest score.

2   Colour in the house points table according to these instructions:

(a)   For Year 3 colour the days that are above its mean.

(b)   For Year 4 use a different colour to shade the days that are below the median.

(c)   For Year 5 use a third colour to shade the days that are below the mode.

3   For Year 6, how many days are:

(a)   above its mode?   ....

(b)   above its median?   ....

(c)   above its mean?   ....

Unit A6/11 Problems with area of composite shapes, volume and time intervals

PNS Framework objectives

- Suggest, plan and develop lines of enquiry; collect, organise and represent information, interpret results and review methods; identify and answer related questions.
- Calculate the perimeter and area of rectilinear shapes; estimate the area of an irregular shape by counting squares.

Unit learning outcome

- To solve problems with area of composite shapes and volume.

Prior knowledge

- This unit relates to work covered in Measurement units M6/1 to M6/3.
- Able to use a calculator with decimal numbers.
- Able to work out area of composite shapes.

Starter activity

- Give the class the challenge of estimating how much paint would be needed to paint the walls and ceiling. First, you need to know the approximate area of the walls and ceiling in m^2, excluding windows, doors, cupboards, etc. Then, using a rough paint coverage guide of 1 litre covering $10\,m^2$, divide the area by 10 to estimate how many litres of paint. Round this up to the next multiple of 5 to decide how many five-litre tins would have to be bought.

Answers to A6/11

1 Front end walls: 0.6 litres, back end wall: 0.4 litres, window wall: 0.6 litres
   Inside wall: 1 litre, ceiling: 0.9 litres
2 (a) 3.5 litres (b) 7 litres
3 Two 5-litre tins will be needed

Unit A6/11 Problems with area of composite shapes, volume and time intervals

Alison has decided to paint the walls and ceiling of her attic bedroom yellow. The walls and ceiling are odd shapes so she drew them to work out how much paint she needs. On the 5-litre tin of paint it says that it will cover 55 m².

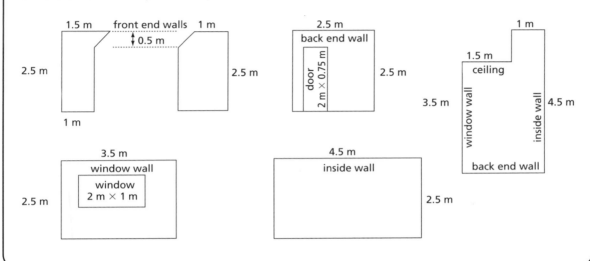

1   If 1 litre of paint covers 11 m², how much paint is needed for each section?
    front end walls: ....   back end wall: ....   window wall: ....
    inside wall: ....   ceiling: ....
2   How much paint will she need altogether:
    (a)   for one coat of paint? ....   (b)   for two coats of paint? ....
3   How many 5-litre tins of paint will she need for two coats of paint? ....

Unit A6/12 Problems with shape and rotational symmetry

PNS Framework objectives

- Suggest, plan and develop lines of enquiry; collect, organise and represent information, interpret results and review methods; identify and answer related questions.
- Use co-ordinates in the first quadrant to draw, locate and complete shapes that meet given properties.

Unit learning outcome

- To solve problems with shape and rotational symmetry.

Prior knowledge

- This unit relates to work covered in Shape units S6/1 to S6/8.
- Able to use a protractor to measure angles and to draw angles of a specified size.

Starter activities

- Borrow large construction nuts and bolts from Early Years/Key Stage 1 (e.g. Mecaniko® or Technico®) and demonstrate how the rotational symmetry of the hexagonal nuts makes it easier to apply a spanner to tighten them. (Use thumb and forefinger to represent a spanner.)
- Use a four-quadrant grid (like the one on the sheet) to make a simple design to pass on to a partner as a set of co-ordinates.

Answers to A6/12

1 (a) Triangle or pentagon
  (c) 3 or 5 depending on the shape chosen

(b) Drawing of either triangle or pentagon

2

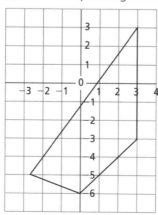

3 (a) Drawing of a parallelogram
  (b) Angles of 95°, 95°, 85° and 85°
  (c) Opposite angles are equal

Unit A6/12 Problems with shape and rotational symmetry

A scientist has invented a machine that makes cabbage taste nice.

He is worried that people might unscrew the bolts with a spanner to see how it works.

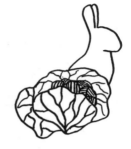

1   To solve this he makes special-shaped bolts and one special tool that will fit over to fasten them.
    To be 'spanner-proof' the bolt heads must not have any parallel edges.

   (a)   Draw a circle around the shapes that are spanner-proof:

      square   triangle   oblong
      pentagon   hexagon

   (b)   Choose one of the spanner-proof shapes and draw it in this box.

   (c)   How many times will it fit into its outline in one complete turn of the bolt? ....

2   He uses a secret code to disguise the design for his spanner-proof bolts. Here is his coded design: (3, 3), (0, −1), (3, −3), (−2½, −5), (0, −6). Use this grid to draw his secret design.

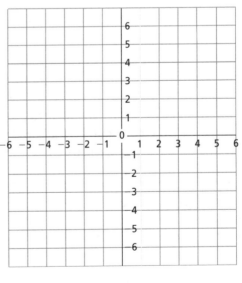

3   The machine is *almost* a cuboid shape. To make it hard to copy, each face of the cuboid has one angle of 95°, making each face a parallelogram.

   (a)   Draw what one face of the machine *might* look like.

   (b)   What are the other three angles of the face you have drawn? ....

   (c)   What do you notice about the angles? ....

Unit S5/1 Quadrilaterals

PNS Framework objective

- Identify, visualise and describe properties of rectangles, triangles, regular polygons and 3-D solids; use knowledge of properties to draw 2-D shapes, and to identify and draw nets of 3-D shapes.

Unit learning outcomes

- To recognise, name and classify quadrilaterals.
- To understand the relationships between different quadrilaterals.

Prior knowledge

- Able to recognise right angles.

Starter activity

- Use strips of paper or card to make quadrilaterals by making three folds and joining the ends together like this:

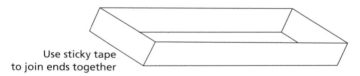

Use sticky tape to join ends together

Use a ruler to compare the length of sides to see if the shape is a regular quadrilateral or a trapezium. Use a set square or similar right-angled shape to decide whether or not the shape is rectangular. Adjust the folds to change the angles of the corners, for example to change a parallelogram into a rectangle and vice versa. Compare the lengths of opposite pairs of sides to see if the shape is a square or rhombus.

Answers to S5/1

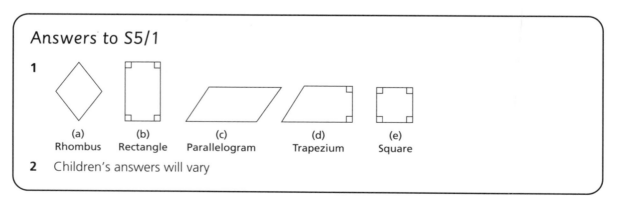

1

| (a) | (b) | (c) | (d) | (e) |
| Rhombus | Rectangle | Parallelogram | Trapezium | Square |

2 Children's answers will vary

Unit S5/1 Quadrilaterals

Here are some clues to help you with this unit:
Equal sides means sides that are the same length
Opposite sides means 2 sides facing each other, not touching
Parallel means lines that stay the same distance apart
Right angles are square corners of 90°, like the corners of a page

S5/1

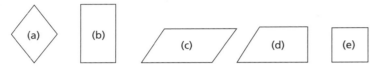

Right angles are often marked like this one ⟶

1   Label these shapes and mark right angles as shown above.

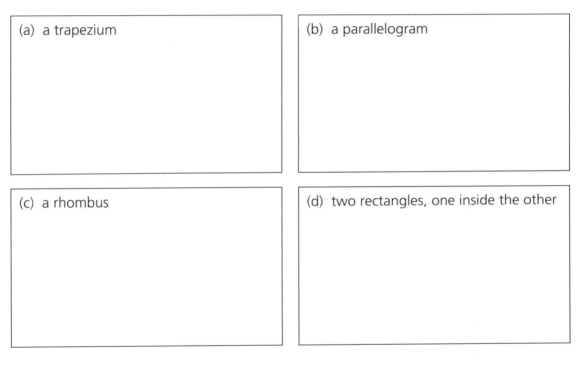

(a)   (b)   (c)   (d)   (e)

2   Draw the following inside these frames:

(a) a trapezium

(b) a parallelogram

(c) a rhombus

(d) two rectangles, one inside the other

Challenge

Draw some more shapes, but only using right angles (90°) and ½ right angles (45°).

Unit S5/2 Triangles

PNS Framework objective

- Identify, visualise and describe properties of rectangles, triangles, regular polygons and 3-D solids; use knowledge of properties to draw 2-D shapes, and to identify and draw nets of 3-D shapes.

Unit learning outcome

- To recognise, name and classify triangles.

Prior knowledge

- Can recognise right angles and can use a ruler precisely enough to compare the length of sides to see if they are equal.

Starter activity

- Use scrap paper and random cutting to make a number of triangles. Pick out any that look as if they may have a right angle. Fold an irregular-shaped piece of paper in half then fold the fold in half to form a right angle. Use this to check if the picked-out triangles do have a right angle or not. Now cut out triangles that do have right angles by cutting rectangles diagonally in half.

Answers to S5/2

1 (a) Right-angled scalene   (b) Equilateral
   (c) Right-angled isosceles   (d) Isosceles
   (e) Right-angled scalene   (f) Scalene
   (g) Equilateral   (h) Right-angled scalene
2 Answers will vary

Unit S5/2 Triangles

Here are some clues to help you with this sheet:

In a *scalene* triangle all three sides are different lengths and all three angles are different.

A *right-angled* triangle has one angle that is a right angle, 90°.

An *equilateral* triangle has all three sides the same length, and each angle is 60°.

An *isosceles* triangle has two sides that are equal and two angles are equal. The third angle could be a right angle, making it a *right-angled isosceles triangle*.

1   Name these triangles:

(a)   ....

(b)   ....

(c)   ....

(d)   ....

(e)   ....

(f)   ....

(g)   ....

(h)   ....

2   Draw the following triangles inside these frames:

(a) a scalene triangle with one side 5 cm and one 7 cm long

(b) a right-angled isosceles triangle

(c) an isosceles triangle *without* a right angle

(d) a right-angled scalene triangle with sides of 3 cm, 4 cm and 5 cm

Challenge

Draw and cut out right-angled isosceles triangles. See if they will fit together without leaving gaps.

Unit S5/3 Polyhedra

PNS Framework objectives

- Describe, identify and visualise parallel and perpendicular edges or faces; use these properties to classify 2-D shapes and 3-D solids.
- Make and draw shapes with increasing accuracy and apply knowledge of their properties.

Unit learning outcome

- To recognise, name and classify polyhedra, including prisms.

Prior knowledge

- Familiar with names of common 2-D shapes.
- Correctly uses the terms 'face' and 'edge' as applied to the properties of 3-D shapes.

Starter activities

- Look at commercially made solid shapes and count the faces. Compare the shape of each face. Look at a cone and a sphere – use the first sentence of the worksheet to decide if they are polyhedra.
- Look at a collection of card boxes (e.g. from breakfast cereals, tea bags, etc.) and carefully prise them apart to look at the net which formed them.

Answers to S5/3

1 (a) Triangular prism   (b) Triangular-based pyramid   (c) Hexagonal prism
   (d) Square-based pyramid   (e) Cuboid (or square prism)   (f) Triangular prism
   (g) Cube   (h) Cuboid   (i) Cuboid
2 Answers will vary

Unit S5/3 Polyhedra

A *polyhedron* is a solid shape made up of flat surfaces. The plural of polyhedron is *polyhedra*. Here are some clues to help you identify polyhedra.

Cubes have 6 square faces.

Cuboids: If it has 6 rectangular faces, it is a cuboid.

Prisms are the same shape and size all the way through so that its cross-sections are the same as the two ends. The shape of the two ends gives it its name, e.g. a triangular prism.

Pyramids have a flat base and triangular faces which join together to make a point (called an *apex*). The shape of the base gives it its name, e.g. if the base is square it is called a square-based pyramid.

1 Name these polyhedra:

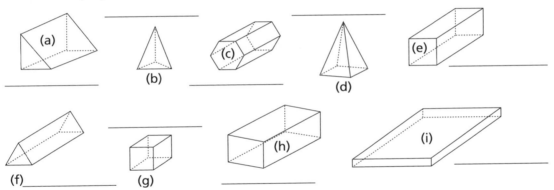

2 Make 3-D drawings of these polyhedra:

(a) a cube	(b) a cuboid with two square faces
(c) a pentagonal prism	(d) a triangular pyramid

Challenge

Make a list of as many things as you can that are cuboid-shaped. Who in your group can think of the most?

S5/4 Line symmetry

PNS Framework objective

- Complete patterns with up to two lines of symmetry; draw the position of a shape after a reflection or translation.

Unit learning outcome

- To understand and use line symmetry.

Prior knowledge

- Understands simple reflective symmetry in objects.

Starter activities

- In pairs play 'Match it'. Each pair needs a grid with a symmetry line mark on and a supply of differently coloured cubes. One player places a cube on his side of the grid then counts slowly to ten while the other matches with a cube of the same colour in a corresponding position. The second player then adds another cube and gives the first player a count of ten to respond. After each pair of turns, the time limit is reduced by one. The first player to make a mistake or run out of time loses. Vary the game by changing the position of the symmetry line and by allowing players to place their cube on either side of it.
- Use computer software and the interactive whiteboard to make symmetrical shapes by copying and flipping the image and joining the two parts together. Try with MS Paint.
- Open a photograph of a person's face in MS Paint or MS Publisher. Split the image down the centre of the nose. (To do this in Publisher you need to make a copy and crop half of each copy.) Start with one half of the face and copy it, flip the copy and join it on to make a symmetrical face. Do the same with the other half of the picture, the results can be very different.

Answers to S5/4

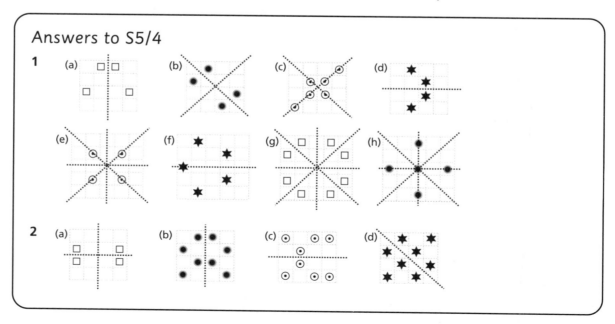

S5/4 Line symmetry

If a shape can be folded exactly in half, we say it is *symmetrical*.

The line of the fold is called the *axis of symmetry*.

This shape has two axes of symmetry. One half is a reflection of the other. If you place a mirror down the line of symmetry the shape will look complete.

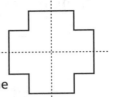

We can make symmetrical patterns with objects like these by placing them on a grid.

 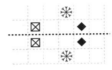

1   Draw in all the axes of symmetry for these patterns:

(a)   (b)   (c)   (d)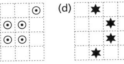

(e) 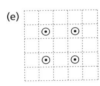   (f) 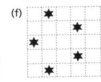   (g) 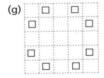   (h)

2   Complete these patterns to make them symmetrical:

(a)   (b)   (c)   (d)

Challenge

Make up a symmetrical pattern of your own using an 8 _ 8 square grid.

Unit S5/5 Translating and rotating shapes

PNS Framework objective

- Complete patterns with up to two lines of symmetry; draw the position of a shape after a reflection or translation.

Unit learning outcome

- To translate and rotate shapes and understand the effect.

Prior knowledge

- Able to read two-figure co-ordinates.
- Understands terms 'rotate', 'clockwise' and 'anticlockwise'.

Starter activities

- Ask a volunteer to stand up in the classroom. Tell them that they must remain facing the same direction. The rest of the class are to give verbal instructions to guide the volunteer to another part of the room, avoiding obstructions. Instructions are given in number of steps forwards, backwards, left and right. Record the moves on the whiteboard and total up moves taken in each direction. Look at the totals – if there are any opposite moves, i.e. both left and right, find the overall movement by taking the smaller total away from the larger. Replicate the movement on a grid on the whiteboard showing two movements, one forward or back and one left or right. Point out that while the position has changed, the direction they were facing has not.
- Ask another volunteer to stand up in a space with one foot on a marked spot. Tell them that they must keep their foot on that same spot. Ask someone to give them an instruction to make them face another feature of the room. The format for instructions is 'rotate' $\frac{1}{4}$, $\frac{1}{2}$, or $\frac{3}{4}$ 'of a turn'/'clockwise' or 'anticlockwise'. The volunteer can also extend an arm forwards to accentuate the turning motion.

Answers to S5/5

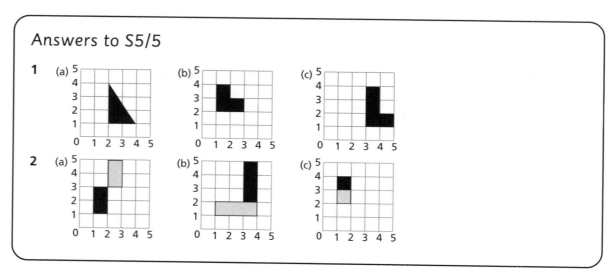

Unit S5/5 Translating and rotating shapes

This oblong has been placed on a grid

It can be translated (moved)

And it can be rotated

(a)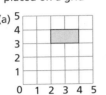

(b)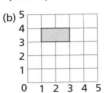

(c)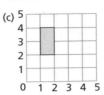

S5/5

1   Translate these shapes:

(a) Translate this shape one square to the left

(b) Translate this 1 square left and 1 square up

(c) Translate this 2 squares right and 1 square down

This shape has been rotated ¼ of a turn clockwise around the point (3, 2)

2   Rotate these shapes:

(a) Rotate this oblong ½ of a turn clockwise around (2, 3)

(b) Rotate this oblong ¼ of a turn clockwise around (4, 2)

(c) Rotate this square ¼ of a turn clockwise around (2, 3)

Challenge

Draw a grid on both large- and small-squared paper. Cut out a shape and place it on the large-squared grid and draw it on the small-squared grid. Rotate the cut-out shape and draw its new position on the grid, using a different colour. Repeat this rotation and drawing until the shape is back in its original position.

Unit S5/6 Co-ordinates

PNS Framework objective

- Read and plot co-ordinates in the first quadrant; recognise parallel and perpendicular lines in grids and shapes; use a set square and ruler to draw shapes with perpendicular or parallel sides.

Unit learning outcome

- To read and plot co-ordinates in the first quadrant.

Prior knowledge

- Understands that 'co-ordinates' means 'two directions' and is used to locate positions on a grid.
- Knows that the numbers relate to the grid lines.
- Knows the convention of recording the x-axis first and then the y-axis.

Starter activities

- Show a co-ordinate grid on the whiteboard and draw a simple house design on it using the intersections of grid lines for all of the angles of the drawing. Ask children for the co-ordinates of the roof, door, chimney, front wall, etc.
- In pairs, using an identical co-ordinate grid, each child in turn marks something on their hidden grid and asks their partner to mark it on theirs using verbal instructions and co-ordinates. After several turns each they compare their grids to check that they both have the same.

Answers to S5/6

1

a (12, 9)	b (3, 7)	c (16, 6)	d (5, 1)	e (13, 2)	f (15, 5)	g (10, 1)	h (15, 7)
i (13, 4)	j (16, 1)	k (7, 10)	l (4, 5)	m (8, 3)	n (6, 6)	o (12, 8)	p (11, 1)
q (9, 4)	r (3, 9)	s (1, 8)	t (4, 8)	u (2, 5)	v (14, 10)	w (5, 6)	x (16, 9)
y (13, 3)	z (12, 4)						

2 Why not make a copy of this on tracing paper or on a clear acetate sheet to place over the children's worksheets for easy marking?

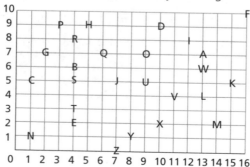

Unit S5/6 Co-ordinates

We can mark positions on a grid using *co-ordinates*.
Two numbers are used, each one giving the position in one direction.

The position in a horizontal direction is given by the *x*-axis.
The position in a vertical direction is given by the *y*-axis.

The area between these two axes is called the *first quadrant*.
We always give the x-axis value first, then the y-axis value like this: *(5, 2)*.

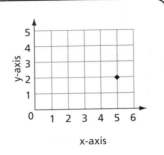

1   Write down the co-ordinates of the letters that are in the first quadrant below.

a .... b .... c ....
d .... e .... f ....
g .... h .... i ....
j .... k .... l ....
m .... n .... o ....
p .... q .... r ....
s .... t .... u ....
v .... w .... x ....
y .... z ....

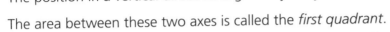

2   Use these co-ordinates to mark these letters on the grid below.

A (13, 7) **B** (4, 6)   **C** (1, 5)   **D** (10, 9)
E (4, 2)   **F** (16, 10) **G** (2, 7)   **H** (5, 9)
I (12, 8) **J** (7, 5)   **K** (15, 5) **L** (13, 4)
M (14, 2) **N** (1, 1)   **O** (9, 7)   **P** (3, 9)
Q (6, 7)   **R** (4, 8)   **S** (4, 5)   **T** (4, 3)
U (9, 5)   **V** (11, 4) **W** (13, 6) **X** (10, 2)
Y (8, 1)   **Z** (7, 0)

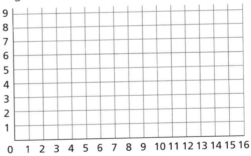

Challenge

Try using a grid of your own to put a message into code. Simply give the co-ordinates of the letters you want. For spaces use a different 'empty' position each time to disguise how long each word is.

Unit S5/7 Angles

PNS Framework objective

- Estimate, draw and measure acute and obtuse angles using an angle measurer or protractor to a suitable degree of accuracy; calculate angles in a straight line.

Unit learning outcomes

- To make and measure angles in degrees.
- To classify angles as acute or obtuse.

Prior knowledge

- Knows how to use a protractor to measure angles.
- Can recognise a right angle and knows that right angles measure 90°.

Starter activities

- Prepare a set of cards with acute, obtuse and right angles (in multiples of 5°) drawn on one side and the measurement discretely written on the reverse. Divide the group into two teams. Shuffle them up. First of all ask teams to call out if a card is a right angle and show the cards one at a time, awarding a point to the team that correctly calls out first. A wrong call earns a point for the other team. Shuffle the cards and repeat, asking them to call out for acute angles; then again for obtuse angles.
- Using the same set of cards ask both teams to estimate the size of the angle and award 1 point for within ±10°, 2 points for within ±5° and 5 points for exactly right.

Answers to S5/7

1 and **2**

(a) 30° coloured red	(b) 50° coloured red	(c) 75° coloured red
(d) 120° coloured blue	(e) 30° coloured red	(f) 150° coloured blue
(g) 85° coloured red	(h) 155° coloured blue	(i) 60° coloured red
(j) 100° coloured blue	(k) 45° coloured red	(l) 135° coloured blue
(m) 40° coloured red	(n) 120° coloured blue	(o) 45° coloured red

Unit S5/7 Angles

When you use a protractor to measure an angle it is very important to line it up correctly.

Protractors usually have a scale numbered in both directions, so make sure you read the scale that starts at 0.

If you are reading off the scale printed on the inside of the protractor, you can still use the outer scale's one-degree markings.

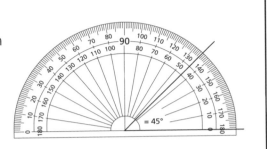

= 45°

1   Measure these angles and mark them on the diagrams.

If an angle is *less than 90°* we say it is *acute*. If it is *more than 90°* but less than 180° we say it is *obtuse*. We can usually tell by just looking.

2   Colour the acute angles red and the obtuse angles blue.

Challenge

Draw a few random angles of your own with a partner; both of you estimate each angle then measure to see how close you both were.

Unit S5/8 Angles on a straight line

PNS Framework objective

- Estimate, draw and measure acute and obtuse angles using an angle measurer or protractor to a suitable degree of accuracy; calculate angles in a straight line.

Unit learning outcome

- To measure and calculate angles on a straight line.

Prior knowledge

- Able to measure angles with a protractor, both clockwise and anticlockwise.

Starter activity

- Split the group up into two teams and assign half of the whiteboard to each. A player from each team is asked to draw their estimation of an angle of less than 180° on their half of the whiteboard. Measure each and award points to the teams for accuracy: award 1 point for within 20°, 2 points for within 10°, 5 points for within 5° and 10 points for within 2°.

Answers to S5/8

1	a = 40°, b = 140°	**2**	a = 60°, b = 120°	**3**	a = 85°, b = 95°
4	a = 120°, b = 60°	**5**	a = 65°, b = 115°	**6**	a = 130°, b = 50°
7	a = 20°, b = 160°	**8**	a = 95°, b = 85°	**9**	a = 115°, b = 65°
10	a = 80°, b = 100°	**11**	a = 150°, b = 30°	**12**	a = 45°, b = 135°

Unit S5/8 Angles on a straight line

Here is a horizontal line with a second line perpendicular to it, making two right angles. One of the two right angles has been marked with a □.

One right angle measures 90°, so two together must equal 180°.

If we angle the perpendicular line over, one of the angles will become smaller while the other becomes bigger.

Angles like these that are on a straight line always add up to 180°.

When we know one angle, we can subtract it from 180° to find the other angle.

For each of these pairs of angles, measure the one marked **a**, and calculate **b** by subtracting it from 180°. Write the measurements on the illustrations.

1
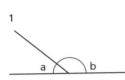

2
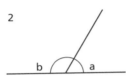

3
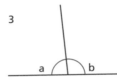

4
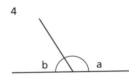

5
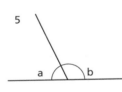

6
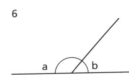

7
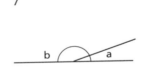

8
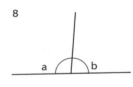

9
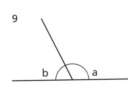

10
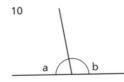

11
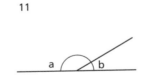

12
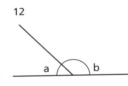

Challenge

Draw a few pairs of angles on a straight line. With a partner, both of you estimate each angle. Check by measuring one of the pair and by calculating the other by subtracting from 180°.

Unit S6/1 Polygons

PNS Framework objectives

- Describe, identify and visualise parallel and perpendicular edges or faces; use these properties to classify 2-D shapes and 3-D solids.
- Make and draw shapes with increasing accuracy and apply knowledge of their properties.

Unit learning outcome

- To recognise, name and classify polygons using mathematical language.

Prior knowledge

- Can recognise and measure right angles.
- Can categorise shapes according to their properties.

Starter activity

- Use a set of flash cards with shapes on to play 'Snap', with the class divided into teams. Award points for correctly snapping and deduct points for errors. Introduce bonus points for those who can give a more precise name to some of the shapes, e.g. right-angled isosceles triangle, regular hexagon.

Answers to S6/1

1 Right angles marked as below

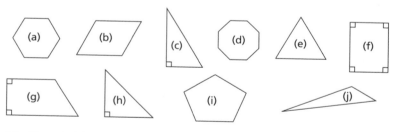

2

(a) (Regular) hexagon
(b) Parallelogram
(c) Right-angled scalene triangle
(d) (Regular) octagon
(e) Equilateral triangle
(f) Oblong (or rectangle)
(g) Trapezium
(h) Right-angled isosceles triangle
(i) (Regular) pentagon
(j) Scalene triangle

Unit S6/1 Polygons

Polygons are flat, closed shapes with straight edges. Their names tell us the number of sides and angles. 'Polygon' means 'many' angles.

You need to understand these terms to complete this unit:

> parallel: lines which remain the same distance apart
> regular: the sides of the shape are equal and the angles are equal
> *right angle*: a 'square' angle of 90°
> *quadrilateral*: a polygon with four sides. Here are some types of quadrilateral:

With right angles	Without right angles
A rectangle has 2 pairs of parallel sides **A square** is a rectangle with all 4 sides equal **An oblong** is a rectangle with opposite sides equal	**A rhombus** has 4 equal sides **A parallelogram** has 2 pairs of parallel sides **A trapezium** has 1 pair of parallel sides

Here are some types of triangle:

Equilateral triangle	all three sides are equal, and all three angles are equal, 60°.
Isosceles triangle	two sides are equal and two angles are equal, and may have a right angle.
Scalene triangle	all three sides are different, and all three angles are different.
Right-angled triangle	one of the angles is a right angle.

The first letters of the names of shapes tell us how many sides and angles they have:
tri = 3, quad = 4, penta = 5, hexa = 6, hepta = 7, octa = 8, deca = 10

1   Mark all the right angles in the shapes below like this:

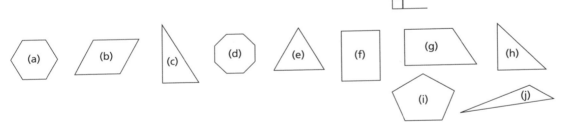

2   Name the shapes shown above.

(a) ....   (b)..

(c) ....   (d)..

(e) ....   (f) ....

(g) ....   (h)..

(i) ....   (j) ....

Challenge

Draw a polygon that is *mentioned* on this sheet but not shown.

Unit S6/2 Polyhedra

PNS Framework objectives

- Describe, identify and visualise parallel and perpendicular edges or faces; use these properties to classify 2-D shapes and 3-D solids.
- Make and draw shapes with increasing accuracy and apply knowledge of their properties.

Unit learning outcome

- To recognise, name and classify polyhedra using mathematical language.

Prior knowledge

- Understands the language of solid shape: 'opposite', 'face', 'edge', 'curved', 'flat', 'cube', 'cuboid', 'prism', 'pyramid'.

Starter activity

- Place an assortment of solid shapes in a box or bag and keep some more hidden from view. Blindfold a volunteer and challenge them to see how many shapes they can remove and identify by touch in 20 seconds. Repeat with several more volunteers; but change some of the shapes. For added interest ask some volunteers to try while wearing gloves or mittens. Practise the language of solid shape and introduce the term 'vertex' (plural: vertices) for the tip of the pyramid and cone.

Answers to S6/2

1 (a) B, D, E, F, G, J, K and L   (b) D and K   (c) G, J and L   (d) A and H
  (e) F   (f) C and I   (g) E   (h) C and I   (i) A and H   (j) B

2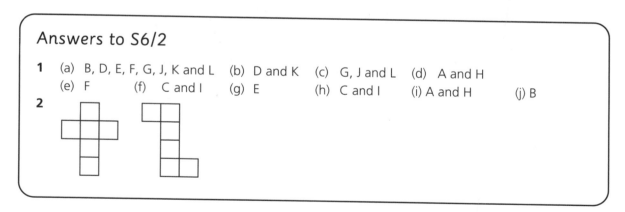

Unit S6/2 Polyhedra

A polyhedron is a solid shape made up of flat faces.

The number and shape of the faces helps us to recognise what sort it is.

Here are some clues:

Cuboids have 6 rectangular faces.

A *prism* has two ends shaped the same, with rectangles in between. Prisms are named after the end shape, e.g. a triangular prism.

A *cylinder* is a circular prism.

A *pyramid* starts with a base shape and rises to a point.

A *cone* is a circular pyramid.

1   Here is a set of polyhedra.

Which:

    (a)   have only flat faces?   ....

    (b)   have 5 faces?   ....

    (c)   have 6 faces?   ....

    (d)   only have 2 faces?   ....

    (e)   has 7 faces?   ....

    (f)   have 3 faces?   ....

    (g)   has 8 faces?   ....

    (h)   will roll straight?   ....

    (i)   will roll in a circle?   ....

    (j)   shape has 4 faces?   ....

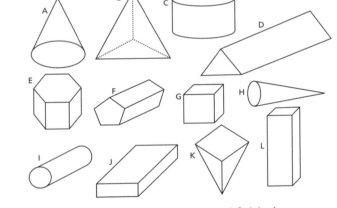

2   Colour the two shapes that will form the *net* of a cube when cut out and folded.

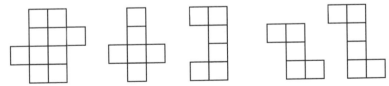

Challenge

Design the net of a cuboid, a triangular prism and a square pyramid.

Cut them out and see if they work.

Unit S6/3 Reflection, rotation and translation

PNS Framework objective

- Visualise and draw on grids of different types where a shape will be after reflection, after translation, or after rotation through 90° or 180° about its centre or one of its vertices.

Unit learning outcome

- To understand where a shape will be after reflection, rotation or translation, or after a combination of rotation and translation.

Prior knowledge

- Able to use co-ordinates to identify points on a grid.

Starter activities

- Stick two differently coloured sheets of sugar paper together back to back and cut out a number of shapes made up of straight lines and right angles. Place these one at a time on a large grid and demonstrate: translation (sliding them up/down/sideways while maintaining their orientation); rotation around a point on the grid (by quarters of a turn, clockwise and anticlockwise); and reflection (flipping horizontally or vertically).
- Use a computer program such as MS PowerPoint or Publisher to demonstrate translation, rotation and reflection. When doing this it is best to copy/drag the shape and re-colour the copy to distinguish the original shape/position from the new.

Answers to S6/3

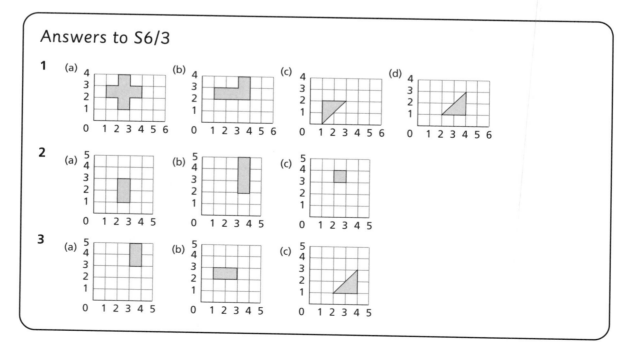

Unit S6/3 Reflection, rotation and translation

This shape has been placed on a grid

It can be 'translated' (moved)

It can be rotated. Here it has been rotated ¼ turn clockwise around (3, 2)

It can be reflected (flipped over)

S6/3

1   Transform these shapes on the grids below as instructed.

(a) Translate this shape one square to the left
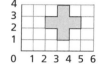

(c) Rotate this shape ¼ turn clockwise around (1, 2)
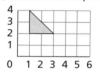

(b) Translate this shape 1 square left and 1 square up

(d) Reflect this shape to the left

2   Try these rotations.

(a) ½ turn anticlockwise around (2, 3)
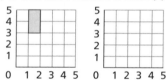

(b) ¼ turn clockwise around (4, 2)
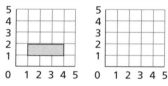

(c) ½ turn clockwise around (2, 3)
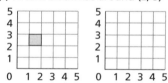

3   These need to be rotated and translated.

(a) ¼ turn clockwise around (2, 3) and translate 2 squares to the right

(b) ¼ turn anticlockwise around (4, 3) and translate 1 square down and 1 square left

(c) ¼ turn anticlockwise around (3, 3) and translate 1 square to the right
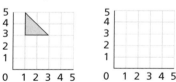

Challenge

Cut out some shapes, place them on a grid and practise translating, reflecting and rotating them.

You can record what you have tried by drawing.

Unit S6/4 Rotational symmetry

PNS Framework objectives

- Describe, identify and visualise parallel and perpendicular edges or faces; use these properties to classify 2-D shapes and 3-D solids.
- Visualise and draw on grids of different types where a shape will be after reflection, after translation, or after rotation through 90° or 180° about its centre or one of its vertices.

Unit learning outcome

- To understand rotational symmetry.

Prior knowledge

- Understands the term 'rotation'.

Starter activity

- Cut out a square in card and mark one edge with an arrow. Find its centre by drawing diagonals. Draw its outline on a sheet of paper on a display board, then pin it on to the outline with the arrow upright. Rotate the square and count how many times it fits into its outline before the arrow returns to the top. Repeat the procedure for an oblong, equilateral triangle, regular pentagon and hexagon. Introduce the term *rotational symmetry* to explain the phenomenon that it *looks* the same when rotated, even though it has not necessarily returned to its starting point. Discuss that many things that are designed to be turned, e.g. screw and bolt heads, have rotational symmetry.

Answers to S6/4

1 (a) 8 (b) 3 (c) 5 (d) 4 (e) 2 (f) 4 (g) 3 (h) 2
2 and **3** Answers will vary

Unit S6/4 Rotational symmetry

Some shapes and objects have *rotational symmetry*. This means that if they are rotated, they will fit back into their original outline. Most things that are designed to turn, like wheels, have rotational symmetry.

Here is a picture of a wheel nut. It has one-sixth turn rotational symmetry because it will fit back into its outline with just one-sixth of a turn. There are 360° in one complete turn so we can also say that it has 60° rotational symmetry.

S6/4

1   Each of these shapes and objects has rotational symmetry. How many times will they fit into their outline in one complete turn? ....

(a)
.... times

(b)
.... times

(c)
.... times

(d)
.... times

(e)
.... times

(f)
.... times

(g)
.... times

(h)
.... times

2   (a)   Draw a simple shape that has rotational symmetry in this box.

(b)   This shape will fit into its outline .... times in one complete rotation.

3   Many things we use in the home or in school have rotational symmetry. Make a list of ten. Examples: pencils, bottle lids, electric fans.

   ....

Challenge

Find three objects in the classroom that have rotational symmetry. Draw them and say how many times they will fit into their outline in one complete turn.

Unit S6/5 Co-ordinates

PNS Framework objective

- Use co-ordinates in the first quadrant to draw, locate and complete shapes that meet given properties.

Unit learning outcome

- To read and plot co-ordinates in all four quadrants.

Prior knowledge

- Able to identify co-ordinates in the first quadrant.
- Able to order positive and negative numbers.

Starter activity

- In pairs, children make a simple first-quadrant grid. While one partner looks away the other draws a simple design, using lines joining up grid positions, and gives the co-ordinates orally for their partner to draw on their grid.

Answers to S6/5

1 A (–3, 4)   B (3, –4)   C (–3, –4)   D (3, 4)   E (2, 4)

F (4, –5)   G (–2, 1)   H (1, –1)   I (5, –3)   J (–4, 3)

2 and **3**

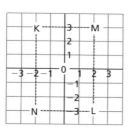

4   An oblong/ a rectangle
5   They mirror each other/they use the same pair of numbers/the numbers are the same but some are positive and some are negative

---

Unit S6/5 Co-ordinates

We can mark positions on a grid using *co-ordinates*.

Two numbers are used, each one giving the position in one direction.

The position in a horizontal direction is given by the x-axis.

The position in a vertical direction is given by the y-axis.

We always give the x-axis position first, like this:

(3, 2)

x-axis position,   y-axis position

If we include negative numbers we get four distinct areas called *quadrants*.

1   Write down the co-ordinates of the letters on the grid.

A (…,…)   B (…,…)   C (…,…)   D (…,…)   E (…,…)

F (…,…)   G (…,…)   H (…,…)   I (…,…)   J (…,…)

2   Mark these letters on this grid:

K (−2, 3)   L (2, −3)   M (2, 3)   N (−2, −3)

3   Use a ruler and a coloured pencil to join the letters together.

4   What have you drawn? …………………………………

5   What do you notice about the four sets of co-ordinates that make the shape? …………………………………………………

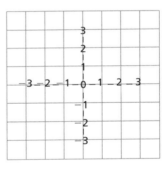

Challenge

Draw a new four-quadrant grid. Choose two numbers that will fit on your grid. Make four sets of co-ordinates using just these two numbers with the help of the minus sign.

Mark them on your four-quadrant grid and see what shape they make.

Unit S6/6 Angles

PNS Framework objective

- Estimate angles and use a protractor to measure and draw them, on their own and in shapes; calculate angles in a triangle or around a point.

Unit learning outcome

- To use a protractor to measure and draw angles to the nearest degree.

Prior knowledge

- Understands that angles are a measure of turn and are measured in degrees.
- Knows that an angle remains constant regardless of the distance from the point where the lines meet.

Starter activity

- Divide the class into two teams. Invite one member of each team to draw an angle of a specified size on half of the whiteboard, without using a protractor. Encourage them to base their estimate on their knowledge of what a right angle and half right angle look like. Measure their efforts with a board protractor and award points to their teams for accuracy: one point for within ±10° and 3 points for within ±5°. When checking, draw attention to counting the single degree markings on the scale.

Answers to S6/6

1 (a) 35°   (b) 135°   (c) 45°   (d) 58°   (e) 112°   (f) 80°
   (g) 97°   (h) 72°
2 To check the drawing of angles more easily, draw and label them on tracing paper or an acetate sheet, then place it over the children's efforts
   (a) 62°   (b) 77°   (c) 84°   (d) 115°   (e) 138°   (f) 148°

Unit S6/6 Angles

When you use a protractor to measure an angle it is very important to line it up correctly.

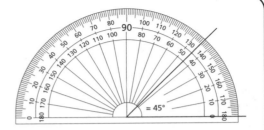

Protractors usually have a scale numbered in both directions, so make sure you read the scale that starts at 0.

If you are reading off the scale printed on the inside of the protractor, you can still use the outer scale's one degree markings.

Before you measure, estimate – is the angle close to, more or less than a right angle (90°)? Is it close to, more or less than a half right angle (45°)?

When you measure, is your reading near your estimate? If not, have you read the correct scale?

1   Estimate these angles *before* you measure them.

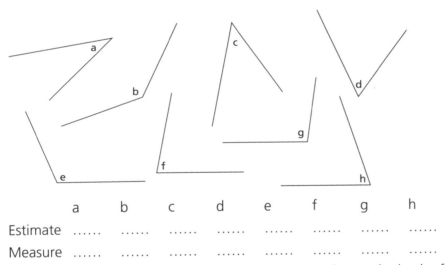

	a	b	c	d	e	f	g	h
Estimate	......	......	......	......	......	......	......	......
Measure	......	......	......	......	......	......	......	......

2   Use a ruler, protractor and pencil to draw these angles on the back of this worksheet.

(a) 62°   (b) 77°   (c) 84°   (d) 115°   (e) 138°   (f) 148°

Challenge

With a partner, draw a few angles and estimate each one.

Measure each one to see whose estimate was closer.

Unit S6/7 Angles on a straight line

PNS Framework objective

- Estimate angles and use a protractor to measure and draw them, on their own and in shapes; calculate angles in a triangle or around a point.

Unit learning outcome

- To calculate angles on a straight line and at a point.

Prior knowledge

- Able to use a protractor with an accuracy of 1°.

Starter activity

- Fold a strip of card in half and place it with one half flat on a table and the other half raised in the air to form an angle. Ask for estimates of the (acute) angle formed between the two halves of the card. Ask for estimates of the (obtuse) angle formed between the raised end of the card and the table top behind the fold. Move the card over to the edge of the table so that both angles can be measured with a protractor. Write the pair of angles down on the whiteboard then repeat with another strip of card which has been folded with a different amount of pressure resulting in a different acute angle. Write the angles down again, 'What do you notice about the two pairs of angles?'.

Answers to S6/7

1 a = 115°, b = 65°	**2** a = 47°, b = 133°	**3** a = 72°, b = 108°	**4** a = 131°, b = 49°
5 b = 156°	**6** b = 91°	**7** b = 147°	**8** b = 126°
9 b = 85°	**10** b = 164°	**11** b = 69°	**12** b = 113°
13 a = 45°, b = 315°	**14** a = 70°, b = 290°	**15** a = 90°, b = 270°	**16** a = 135°, b = 225°

Unit S6/7 Angles on a straight line

Angles that are on a straight line always add up to 180°.

When we know one angle, we can calculate the other by subtracting it from 180°.

135° ⟋ 45°

For each of these pairs of angles measure the one marked **a** *to the nearest degree*, then calculate angle **b** by subtracting angle **a** from 180°.

Example: *angle **a** = 45°,   angle **b** = 180° – 45°, = 135°.*

1. a = ... °   b = ... °   2. a = ... °   b = ... °   3. a = ... °   b = ... °   4. a = ... °   b = ... °

Find angle **b** by subtracting angle **a** from 180°:

  5   **a** = 24° **b** = ...°   6 **a** = 89° **b** = ...°   7 **a** = 33° **b** = ...°

  8   **a** = 54° **b** = ...°   9 **a** = 95° **b** = ...°   10 **a** = 16° **b** = ...°

11   **a** = 111° **b** = ...°   12 **a** = 67° **b** = ...°

We can use this subtraction method to calculate in a complete turn of 360° by subtracting 76° from 360° like this: 360° – 76° = 284°.

Measure the angle marked **a** *to the nearest degree*, then calculate angle **b** by subtracting angle **a** from 180°.

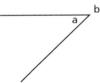

13 a = ... °   b = ... °

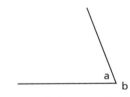

14 a = ... °   b = ... °

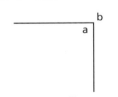

15 a = ... °   b = ... °

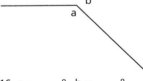

16 a = ... °   b = ... °

Challenge

Draw four more pairs of angles that are 'around a point' like the ones in 13 to 16. Measure the smaller angle and calculate the larger angle. If you have a 360° protractor you can check your calculation by measuring.

Unit S6/8 Angle sums

PNS Framework objective

- Estimate angles and use a protractor to measure and draw them, on their own and in shapes; calculate angles in a triangle or around a point.

Unit learning outcome

- To calculate angles in a triangle and investigate angle sums of regular polygons.

Prior knowledge

- Able to accurately measure angles with a protractor to within 1°.
- Competent with basic addition and subtraction.

Starter activity

- In pairs or individually, ask children to make a triangle on a geoboard using a rubber band. After looking at their efforts, ask them to measure all three angles and write them down. Now ask them to move one of the corners to a different pin and re-measure the angles. Discuss the changes in the angles and arrive at the conclusion that the increase in one or two angles is balanced by a decrease in one or two angles.

Answers to S6/8

1 (a) 45°	(b) 90°	(c) 45°	**2** (a) 90°	(b) 40°	(c) 50°
3 (a) 45°	(b) 30°	(c) 105°	**4** (a) 45°	(b) 50°	(c) 85°

5 180°

6 Children's answers will vary

7 75°

8 45°

9 120°

10 49°

Unit S6/8 Angle sums

Carefully measure the three angles of each triangle.

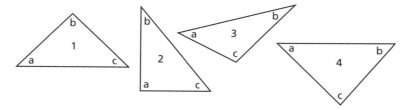

1   a = ... °, b = ... °, c = ... °
2   a = ... °, b = ... °, c = ... °
3   a = ... °, b = ... °, c = ... °
4   a = ... °, b = ... °, c = ... °
5   The three angles of each triangle *should* add up to the same total of .... °
6   Draw a triangle in this box, measure its angles and total them up.

.... ° + ... ° + ... ° = ... °

You should have discovered that the angles in a triangle all add up to 180°.

We can use this to calculate a third angle if we know the other two like this example: *unknown angle = 180° − (35° + 90°), = 180° − 125°, = 55°.*

Use this method to find the unknown angles below.

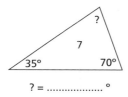

? = ... °

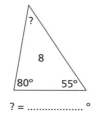

? = ... °

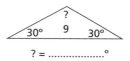

? = ... °

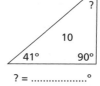

? = ... °

Challenge

Get a regular polygon template (e.g. rectangle, pentagon, hexagon, octagon) and carefully draw around it. Measure *one* angle (the angles are all the same value). Now multiply that angle by the number of angles. What answer do you get?

Unit M5/1 Length, mass and capacity

PNS Framework objective

- Read, choose, use and record standard metric units to estimate and measure length, weight and capacity to a suitable degree of accuracy (e.g. the nearest centimetre); convert larger to smaller units using decimals to one place (e.g. change 2.6 kg to 2600 g).

Unit learning outcomes

- To know and use the relationships between metric units of length, mass and capacity.
- To make approximate conversions from imperial to metric units.

Prior knowledge

- Familiar with metric units of mass, length and volume.
- Able to use place value to divide by 1000.

Starter activities

- Brainstorm different units of mass (weight), volume and length, both metric and imperial. Sort them out according to type or measure and imperial or metric.
- If you have an ICT suite available ask the children in pairs to use a search engine to find as many different imperial units of mass (weight), volume and length as they can. To make the search easier they should put the search phrase 'imperial units' within speech marks and use it in combination with 'mass', 'weight', 'length' or volume, without speech marks. Ask the children to also record an approximate conversion, e.g. '1 fluid ounce = about 30 millilitres'.

Answers to M5/1

1 (a) 300 g (b) 2.65 ml (c) 50 cm (d) 200 ml (e) 250 mm (f) 4250 g
      (g) 600 mm (h) 1.2 kg (i) 750 ml

2 (a) 20 cm (b) 12.5 cm (c) 60 cm (d) 150 cm (e) 40 cm (f) 2 m 18 cm
      (g) 9 m 10 cm (h) 13 m 8 cm (i) 105 cm (j) 9 l (k) 45 l (l) 198 l (m) 1.5 l
      (n) 3 l (o) 5 l (p) 900 g (q) 1.575 kg (r) 3600 g (s) 112 g
      (t) 280 g (u) 224 g

Challenge conversions:
      (a) 20.32 cm (b) 12.7 cm (c) 60.96 cm (d) 152.4 cm (e) 40.64 cm (f) 1.8288 m
      (g) 9.144 m (h) 10.9728 m (i) 106.68 cm (j) 9.092 l (k) 45.46 l
      (l) 200.024 l (m) 1.704 l (n) 3.408 l (o) 5.68 l (p) 0.9072 kg (q) 1.5876 kg
      (r) 3.6288 kg (s) 113.4 g (t) 283.5 g (u) 226.8 g

Unit M5/1 Length, mass and capacity

We can measure length in kilometres (km), metres (m), centimetres (cm) and millimetres (ml).

We can measure mass (weight) in kilograms (kg) and grams (g).

We can measure volume and capacity in litres (l) and millilitres (ml).

Reminders:

1 kilometre = 1000 metres	1 metre = 1000 millimetres	1 metre = 100 centimetres
1 kilogram = 1000 grams	1 litre = 1000 millilitres	

1 Complete these conversions.

(a)   3/10 kg = ... g   (b)   2650 ml = ... l   (c)   1/2 m = ... cm

(d)   1/5 l = ... ml   (e)   1/4 m = ... mm   (f)   4 1/4 kg = ... g

(g)   6/10 m = ... mm   (h)   1200 g = ... kg   (i)   3/4 l = ... ml

Many older people prefer to use the old *Imperial* units of measurement.

Here are some *approximate* conversions, they are not exact but can be used without a calculator!

Length	1 inch is about $2\frac{1}{2}$ cm	1 foot (12 inches) is about 30 cm	1 yard (3 feet) is about 1 m 9 cm
Weight	1 pound (symbol: lb) is about 450 g, just under $\frac{1}{2}$ kg		1 ounce (symbol: oz) is about 28 g
Volume	1 gallon (8 pints) is about $4\frac{1}{2}$ litres		1 pint is just over $\frac{1}{2}$ a litre

2 Use these approximate conversions to change the following into metric units.

(a)   8 inches = ...   (b)   5 inches = ...   (c)   2 feet = ...

(d)   5 feet = ...   (e)   1 foot 4 inches = ...   (f)   2 yards = ...

(g)   10 yards = ...   (h)   12 yards = ...   (i) $3\frac{1}{2}$ feet = ...

(j)   2 gallons = ...   (k)   10 gallons = ...   (l)   44 gallons = ...

(m) 3 pints = ...   (n)   6 pints = ...   (o)   10 pints = ...

(p)   2 lb = ...   (q) $3\frac{1}{2}$ lb = ...   (r)   8 lb = ...

(s)   4 oz = ...   (t)   10 oz = ...   (u)   8 oz = ...

Challenge

Use a calculator and these figures to make more accurate conversions.

Length	1 inch = 2.54 cm	1 foot = 30.48 cm	1 yard = 0.9144 m
Weight	1 ounce = 28.35 g	1 lb = 0.4536 kg	
Volume	1 pint = 0.568 litres	1 gallon = 4.546 litres	

Unit M5/2 How accurate?

PNS Framework objective

- Read, choose, use and record standard metric units to estimate and measure length, weight and capacity to a suitable degree of accuracy (e.g. the nearest centimetre); convert larger to smaller units using decimals to one place (e.g. change 2.6 kg to 2600 g).

Unit learning outcome

- To record measurements to a suitable degree of accuracy.

Prior knowledge

- Familiar with the varied units of measurement listed on the sheet.

Starter activity

- Draw a set of three overlapping Venn diagram rings on the whiteboard and label them 'length', 'weight' and 'volume'. Ask the children to suggest things that could be measured and write them in the appropriate sector of the diagram according to what we would be likely to measure. For example, 'a bus' would most likely be placed in the intersection of 'weight' and 'length' whereas a bottle of sauce might be in the intersection of 'weight' and 'volume'. When you have sufficient items on the diagram discuss with the children how important absolute accuracy might be – the weight of the bus may not be crucial but its length, width and height could affect its manoeuvrability through the bus garage and bus wash.

Answers to M5/2

1 (a) Metres (b) ml (c) km (d) Minutes (e) Weeks or days
   (f) Centuries or years (g) mm (h) kg (i) Minutes (j) Years
   (k) Grams (l) Weeks or days (m) Centuries or millennia (n) Grams
   (o) Tonnes (p) mm (q) ml (r) cm or mm (s) Seconds (t) Litres

   Answers regarding the need for accuracy will vary and be open to discussion

2 (a) 297 mm (b) 210 mm

   The remaining answers will vary

Unit M5/2 How accurate?

When we measure we don't always need to be exact. For example, distances marked on road signs are not accurate to the nearest metre.

Some measurements need to be very accurate, to the nearest millimetre or even closer!

Here are some possible units to choose from:

length: kilometres (km), metres (m), centimetres (cm), millimetres (mm)

weight: tonnes, kilograms, kilos (kg), grams (g)

volume: litres (l), millilitres (ml)

time: millennia, centuries, years, months, weeks, days, hours, minutes ('), seconds (")

1   Below are some things to be measured. Say which units you would use to measure them. Underline the units if the measurement needs to be accurate.

(a) the distance between two goal posts ....

(b) the pop inside a glass ....

(c) the distance between two towns ....

(d) the duration of playtime ....

(e) the length of the school summer holiday ....

(f) the age of a house ....

(g) the thickness of a pencil lead ....

(h) the weight of a dog ....

(i) the duration of an English lesson ....

(j) the age of your teacher ....

(k) the weight of a packet of crisps ....

(l) the age of a baby ....

(m) the age of a dinosaur skeleton ....

(n) the weight of a hamster ....

(o) the weight of an elephant ....

(p) the length of a pin ....

(q) the medicine in a spoonful ....

(r) the length of a pencil ....

(s) the time to run 100 metres ....

(t) the water to fill a bath ....

2   Use a ruler to measure the following, accurate to the nearest millimetre:

(a) the length of a piece of A4 paper ....

(b) the width of a piece of A4 paper ......

(c) the length of a maths text book ....

(d) the width of a maths text book ....

(e) the thickness of an exercise book ....

(f) the length of an exercise book ....

(g) the width an exercise book ....

(h) the width of your ruler ....

(i) the width of your pencil ....

(j) the length of your pencil ....

Challenge

Find a way of measuring the thickness of a piece of paper. Clue: you might need to measure more than one sheet at a time.

Unit M5/3 Area

PNS Framework objective

- Draw and measure lines to the nearest millimetre; measure and calculate the perimeter of regular and irregular polygons; use the formula for the area of a rectangle to calculate the rectangle's area.

Unit learning outcome

- To calculate the areas of rectangles and triangles, using formulae.

Prior knowledge

- Firm understanding that area is a measurement of two-dimensional space.
- Able to multiply with and without the aid of a calculator.

Starter activity

- Using cm² paper, ask children to draw rectangles made up of 6, 12, 24, 25 and 36 squares. When complete, for each size of rectangle ask what size the children used. Point out the different options for most of the sizes and the only option for the 25 cm² rectangle, which is a square rectangle rather than an oblong rectangle.

Answers to M5/3

1	(a) 126 cm²	(b) 400 m²	(c) 16 m²	(d) 384 cm²	(e) 1350 cm²	(f) 6000 cm²
	(g) 160 cm²	(h) 600 cm²	(i) 120 m²	(j) 48 cm²	(k) 64 cm²	(l) 418 mm²
	(m) 1500 m²	(n) 100 mm²				
2	(a) 9 cm²	(b) $7\frac{1}{2}$ cm²	(c) $4\frac{1}{2}$ cm²	(d) 3 cm²	(e) 12 cm²	(f) 12 cm²

Unit M5/3 Area

Area is the amount of flat (two-dimensional) space which something occupies.

We use 'square' units to measure area, such as square metres (m²), square centimetres (cm²).

We use the little ² to mean 'square' because a square has two dimensions, length and width.

Length 6 cm
Width 4 cm

To find the area of this rectangle you could simply count the squares, but it is quicker to do it using this formula: *area = length × breadth*.

To find the area of this rectangle we multiply 6 cm × 4 cm = 24 cm².

M5/3

1   Find the area of these rectangles; take care, they are not all in cm. *You can use a calculator.*

(a) A notepad 14 cm × 9 cm ....   (b) A playground 40 m long, 10 m wide ......

(c) A flowerbed 8 m long, 2 m wide ......   (d) An envelope 24 cm × 16 cm ....

(e) An atlas 45 cm × 30 cm ....   (f) A table top 100 cm long, 60 cm wide ......

(g) An envelope 16 cm × 10 cm ....   (h) A sheet of card 30 cm long, 20 cm wide ...

(i) A lawn 15 m × 8 m ....   (j) An oblong 6 cm wide, 8 cm long ....

(k) An 8 cm square ....   (l) A postage stamp 22 mm × 19 mm ....

(m) A car park 50 m × 30 m ....   (n) The top of a cube, 10 mm square ....

If you cut a rectangle in half diagonally you will get two right-angled triangles.

The area of each of them is half of the area of the rectangle that was cut in half.

You can use this to find the area of right-angled triangles using the sides that form the right angle.

Multiply the two shorter sides together then halve the answer.

Example: (3 cm × 2 cm) = 6 cm², ÷ 2, = 3 cm²

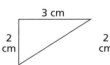

2   Find the area of these right-angled triangles. *You can use a calculator.*

            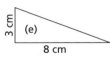

area = ...   area = ...   area = ...   area = ...   area = ...   area = ...

Challenge

Draw some right-angled triangles of your own and calculate their areas.

Unit M5/4 Perimeter

PNS Framework objective

- Draw and measure lines to the nearest millimetre; measure and calculate the perimeter of regular and irregular polygons; use the formula for the area of a rectangle to calculate the rectangle's area.

Unit learning outcome

- To calculate the perimeters of rectangles and triangles, using formulae.

Prior knowledge

- Competent with mental addition including use of short-cut methods.
- Competent with doubling numbers.

Starter activity

- Make a 10 m loop of string and ask three children to stand inside it, pulling it taut to form a triangle. Use a surveyor's tape to measure the three sides to the nearest $\frac{1}{4}$ metre and record on the whiteboard. It may be necessary to 'check' measurements to ensure that the perimeter remains 10 m. Make several more triangles by asking one of the children to move position, and record the sides of these. Confirm that each triangle has the same perimeter, (a) because they all add up to 10 m, and (b) because the same loop of string was used.

  Repeat this procedure using a loop of string that, unknown to the children, is 8 m long. Measure the sides to the nearest $\frac{1}{4}$ metre and confirm the perimeter of each triangle formed.

Answers to M5/4

1 (a) 18 cm   (b) 24 cm   (c) 37 cm   (d) 15 cm   (e) 20 cm   (f) 19 cm
   (g) 18 cm   (h) $30\frac{1}{2}$ cm   (i) $11\frac{3}{4}$ cm   (j) $16\frac{1}{2}$ cm^2

2 (a) 26 cm   (b) 36 cm   (c) 34 cm   (d) 48 m   (e) 20 cm   (f) 60 m
   (g) 32 cm   (h) 70 m   (i) 600 mm   (j) 480 mm   (k) 76 cm   (l) 27 cm
   (m) 50 cm   (n) 24 cm   (o) 51 m   (p) $24\frac{1}{2}$ m

Unit M5/4 Perimeter

The perimeter of a shape is the distance all around its edge. With rectangles and triangles the simplest way to find the perimeter is to add up the lengths of the sides.

Perimeter of triangle = side 1 + side 2 + side 3

Perimeter of rectangle = side 1+ side 2 + side 3 + side 4

With rectangles you can use either of these other methods:

Method 1

$2 \times$ length + $2 \times$ width

$(2 \times 4\,cm) + (2 \times 3\,cm) = 8\,cm + 6\,cm = 14\,cm$

Method 2

length + width $\times$ 2

$(4\,cm + 3\,cm) \times 2 = 14\,cm$

With square rectangles there is an even quicker way because all four sides are the same length: perimeter of square = length of the sides $\times$ 4, $3\,cm \times 4 = 12\,cm$.

1 Work out the perimeter of each of these triangles:

	side 1	side 2	side 3	perimeter		side 1	side 2	side 3	perimeter
(a)	6 cm	5 cm	7 cm	.... cm	(b)	8 cm	8 cm	8 cm	.... cm
(c)	7 cm	14 cm	16 cm	.... cm	(d)	3 cm	7 cm	5 cm	.... cm
(e)	6 cm	6 cm	8 cm	.... cm	(f)	9 cm	4 cm	6 cm	.... cm
(g)	3 cm	4 cm	11 cm	.... cm	(h)	12 cm	10 cm	$8\frac{1}{2}$ cm	.... cm
(i)	4 cm	$3\frac{3}{4}$ cm	$4\frac{1}{2}$ cm	.... cm	(j)	$4\frac{3}{4}$ cm	$8\frac{1}{4}$ cm	$3\frac{1}{2}$ cm	.... cm

2 Use method 1 or method 2 to work out the perimeters of these rectangles measuring:

(a) $8\,cm \times 5\,cm$ = ...

(b) $9\,cm \times 9\,cm$ = ...

(c) $12\,cm \times 5\,cm$ = ...

(d) $20\,m \times 4\,m$ = ...

(e) $7\,cm \times 3\,cm$ = ...

(f) $12\,m \times 18\,m$ = ...

(g) $8\,cm \times 8\,cm$ = ...

(h) $25\,m \times 10\,m$ = ...

(i) $100\,mm \times 200\,mm$ = ...

(j) $120\,mm \times 120\,mm$ = ...

(k) $30\,cm \times 8\,cm$ = ...

(l) $5\frac{1}{2}\,cm \times 8\,cm$ = ...

(m) $12\frac{1}{2}\,cm \times 12\frac{1}{2}\,cm$ = ...

(n) $8\frac{1}{4}\,cm \times 3\frac{3}{4}\,cm$ = ...

(o) $10\frac{1}{2}\,m \times 15\,m$ = ...

(p) $5\frac{1}{2}\,m \times 6\frac{3}{4}\,m$ = ...

Challenge

Find an easy way of working out the perimeters of these regular shapes:

a hexagon with sides 6 cm long ....

an octagon with sides 5 cm long ....

a heptagon with sides 4 cm long ....

a pentagon with sides 8 cm long ....

a decagon with sides 4 cm ....

Unit M5/5 Calendars

PNS Framework objective

- Read timetables and time using 24-hour clock notation; use a calendar to calculate time intervals.

Unit learning outcome

- To understand and use a calendar.

Prior knowledge

- Understands a calendar in tabular form.
- Able to count on weeks from one month to the next.

Starter activities

- Find out and display who was born in each month – which is the commonest? Work out from this who are the oldest members of the group. Which half of the year has more birthdays?
- Find out which is the commonest birthday day of the month.
- Find out which children have birthdays closest to each other.
- Ask children to count on how many months since their last birthday, and how many to their next.

Answers to M5/5

1 (a) and (b)

January	31
February	28 or 29
March	31
April	30
May	31
June	30
July	31
August	31
September	30
October	31
November	30
December	31

2 Answers will vary according to the year

3 Answers will vary according to the year

4 (a) 6 weeks   (b) 19 weeks (c) 14 weeks (d) 6 weeks   (e) 2 weeks   (f) 10 weeks

Unit M5/5 Calendars

We use a calendar to record time in days. We use them to plan ahead, such as when we are going to do something special. On a calendar you can count in months, weeks and days.

M5/5

1 (a) Write down the names of each month in the correct order, be careful with spelling. ⟶

(b) Write down the number of days alongside the names of the months.

2 Look at a calendar for this year.

(a) There are .... Sundays in January this year.

(b) There are .... Sundays in May this year.

(c) There are .... Saturdays in February this year.

(d) There are .... Saturdays in October this year.

3 Here are some incomplete dates, e.g. 16.05 = 16th May. Write the complete date for this year and include which day it falls on.

(a) 30.01 this year is .... day the ...., 20 ....

(b) 02.08 this year is .... day the ...., 20 ....

(c) 15.05 this year is .... day the ...., 20 ....

(d) 14.11 this year is .... day the ...., 20 ....

(e) 25.12 this year is .... day the ...., 20 ....

(f) 14.02 this year is .... day the ...., 20 ....

(g) 23.04 this year is .... day the ...., 20 ....

(h) 28.03 this year is .... day the ...., 20 ....

4 Use a calendar to find out how many weeks there are between:

(a) 1st March and 12th April .... weeks.

(b) 19th June to 30th October .... weeks.

(c) 14th July and 20th October .... weeks.

(d) 16th November and 28th December .... weeks.

(e) 23rd December and 6th January next year .... weeks.

(f) 6th November and 15th January next year .... weeks.

Challenge

Make two copies of the dates for the month you were born in, one copy with the days written across the top, and one copy with the days written down the side.

Unit M5/6 Time and timetables

PNS Framework objective

- Read timetables and time using 24-hour clock notation; use a calendar to calculate time intervals.

Unit learning outcomes

- To read and record times in 24-hour clock notation.
- To use timetables.

Prior knowledge

- Able to tell the time using an analogue clock.

Starter activity

- Ask children what time they do particular things, e.g. bedtime, and write them on the whiteboard exactly as they say them, e.g. 'half eight', '8.30', 'half past eight'. Repeat the process for other times such as when they get up, have a meal, etc. Look at the range of formats written on the whiteboard – which are easier to understand? Which take up less space than others? Which use only numbers? Which show that the time is before or after midday? Decide on a format which would suit all the times shown on the board.

Answers to M5/6

1 (a) 09:00   (b) 19:15   (c) 15:30   (d) 07:15   (e) 17:20
   (f) 19:45   (g) 12:00   (h) 10:30   (i) 09:30   (j) 22:55
   (k) 04:40   (l) 18:25   (m) 06:50   (n) 07:10   (o) 21:45
   (p) 23:59   (q) 00:01   (r) 00:45   (s) 13:15   (t) 20:01

2 Accept any standard 12-hour clock formats (e.g. 'five to seven p.m.' or '6.55 p.m.')

depart	09:35	or	11:05	or	13:45	or	15:20	or	18:55	or
	9.35	a.m.	11.05	a.m.	1.45	p.m.	3.20	p.m.	6.55	p.m.
arrive	10:53	or	12:23	or	15:03	or	16:38	or	20:15	or
	10.53	a.m.	12.23	p.m.	3.03	p.m.	4.38	p.m.	8.15	p.m.

Unit M5/6 Time and timetables

When we write down or say the time we use many ways.

If it is exactly on the hour we say o'clock (o**f the** clock).

Sometimes we say what part of an hour or how many minutes have passed since the last hour, how long before the next hour.

We could say or record this clock's time as:

quarter to 8,

15 minutes to 8,

or 7.45.

This is a *12-hour clock*. When we reach an hour after the middle of the day, we start counting again at 1. The clock face doesn't tell us if it is before or after midday. We use *a.m.* if it's before midday and *p.m.* for after midday.

An easier, neater way to record the time is the *24-hour clock*. We carry on counting the hours so that 1.00 p.m. becomes 13:00, 2 p.m. becomes 14:00 and so on. To keep it simple, use two digits for the hour and two for the minutes past, separated by a colon like this: *07:45*.

1   Change these times to 24-hour clock times.
   If the time is p.m. in the 12-hour clock we add 12 to the hours. 7.15 p.m. = 19:15.
   (a) 9 o'clock a.m. ....   (b) 7.15 p.m. ....   (c) half past 3 p.m. ....
   (d) quarter past 7 a.m. ....   (e) 20 past 5 p.m. ....   (f) quarter to 8 p.m. ......
   (g) 12 noon ....   (h) 10.30 a.m. ....   (i) 9.30 a.m. ....
   (j) 5 to 11 p.m. ....   (k) 20 to 5 a.m. ....   (l) 25 past 6 p.m. ....
   (m) 10 to 7 a.m. ....   (n) 10 past 7 a.m. ....   (o) 9.45 p.m. ....
   (p) 1 minute to midnight ......   (q) 1 minute past midnight ....
   (r) quarter to 1 a.m. ....   (s) $\frac{1}{4}$ past 1 p.m. ....
   (t) 1 minute past 8 p.m. ....

2   Here is a train timetable using 24-hour clock times. Fill in the 12-hour clock times.

depart	09:35	11:05	13:45	15:20	18:55 ....
arrive	10:53	12:23	15:03	16:38	20:15 ....

Challenge

Think about the times of the day that are important to you (when you get up, eat, do things, etc.).

Write down these events and times using both 12- and 24-hour clocks.

Unit M5/7 Time intervals

PNS Framework objective

- Read timetables and time using 24-hour clock notation; use a calendar to calculate time intervals.

Unit learning outcome

- To calculate time intervals.

Prior knowledge

- Able to tell the time in the 24-hour clock format.
- Understands the principle of exchange when subtracting.

Starter activities

- Share with the children what time you leave home to come to school and what time you usually arrive, then ask them how long your journey took. How did they work it out? Did anyone use a different method of working? Do the same for other journeys, real or made up, e.g. travelling to a holiday destination. Again ask the children how they arrived at the correct answer and go through their method(s) on the whiteboard.
- Use a real bus or train timetable (either printed or downloaded from the Internet) and see who is first to find the times of specific journeys.

Answers to M5/7

1. (a) 45 mins (b) 1 hour (c) 4 hours, 15 mins (d) 4 hours, 10 mins
   (e) 8 hours, 35 mins (f) 5 hours, 50 mins (g) 2 hours, 5 mins (h) 2 hours, 50 mins
   (i) 3 hours, 40 mins (j) 50 mins (k) 12 hours, 20 mins (l) 15 hours, 50 mins
2. (a) 4 hours, 10 mins (b) 3 hours, 40 mins (c) 4 hours, 30 mins (d) 1 hour, 50 mins
   (e) 1 hour, 45 mins (f) 2 hours, 50 mins (g) 2 hours, 45 mins (h) 45 mins
   (i) 3 hours, 25 mins (j) 6 hours, 33 mins (k) 6 hours, 1 min (l) 11 hours, 52 mins

Unit M5/7 Time intervals

The simplest way of calculating an interval of time is to 'count on' like this, using 24-hour clock times:

To find the time interval between 09:35 and 12:20,

count on how many minutes to the next hour,	count on the hours,	then add on the minutes.
09:35 + **25** minutes = 10:00	10:00 + **2** hours = 12:00	12:00 + **20** minutes = 12:20

The time interval is **2** hours and (**25 + 20**) minutes = **2 hours**, **45 minutes**.

1   Use this way to work out these time intervals:

      (a) 09:30 to 10:15 ....
      (b) 10:30 to 11:30 ....
      (c) 07:10 to 11:25 ....

      (d) 11:20 to 15:30 ....
      (e) 09:40 to 18:15 ....
      (f) 10:45 to 16:35 ....

      (g) 19:20 to 21:25 ....
      (h) 20:15 to 23:05 ....
      (i) 18:40 to 22:20 ....

      (j) 17:05 to 17:55 ....
      (k) 9:50 to 22:10 ....
      (l) 7:15 to 23:05 ....

You can use subtraction to work out time intervals.

Sometimes you need to exchange an hour like this:

	hours	minutes	
① Exchange 1 hour for 60 minutes	14 ~~15~~ −10	+60 20 50	② 60 mins − 50 mins = 10 mins then add on the other 20 mins = 30
③ Subtract the hours	4	30	

2   Use subtraction to work out these intervals on scrap paper.

      You do not need to exchange for all of them.

      (a) 06:20 to 10:30 ....
      (b) 08:15 to 11:55 ....
      (c) 09:15 to 13:45 ....

      (d) 12:40 to 14:30 ....
      (e) 06:30 to 08:15 ....
      (f) 09:45 to 12:35 ....

      (g) 17:25 to 20:10 ....
      (h) 21:15 to 22:00 ....
      (i) 15:27 to 18:52 ....

      (j) 16:05 to 22:38 ....
      (k) 08:42 to 14:43 ....
      (l) 09:13 to 21:05 ....

Challenge

How could you alter this subtraction method to find intervals of time that go into the next day, for example 22:30 on Monday to 03:40 on Tuesday?

Use the 'counting on' method to check if your way works.

Explain your method to a friend and write out instructions on how to do it.

Unit M6/1 Length, mass and capacity

PNS Framework objective

- Select and use standard metric units of measure and convert between units using decimals to two places (e.g. change 2.75 litres to 2750 ml, or vice versa).

Unit learning outcome

- To know and use relationships between metric units of length, mass and capacity and know common imperial units and metric equivalents.

Prior knowledge

- Confident with metric units of length, volume and mass and can use place value to convert cm to m, ml to l, g to kg, etc.

Starter activities

- Display a mixed-up collection of metric and common imperial units of measure. Ask the children what each is used for measuring (length, volume/capacity, weight) and circle them using different colours of pen to denote what it is used to measure. Ask for suggestions of what might be measured in each unit.

- Ask the children to use a computer search to find other imperial units of measurement for length, volume and weight.

Answers to M6/1

1 (a) 700 g   (b) 400 ml   (c) 900 mm   (d) 5.365 l   (e) 750 mm   (f) 8.205 kg
   (g) 0.7 cm   (h) 2750 g   (i) 250 ml

2 Allow answers that are 'correct' but in either m, cm or mm
   (a) 17.5 cm   (b) 25 cm   (c) 90 cm   (d) 2.7 m   (e) 45 cm   (f) 10.01 m
   (g) 4.55 m   (h) 91 m   (i) 1.8 m

3 Allow answers that are correctly expressed in ml
   (a) 22.5 litres (b) 81 litres   (c) 225 litres (d) 3.5 litres   (e) 6 litres   (f) 12 litres

4 Allow answers that are correctly expressed in kg
   (a) 2250 g   (b) 3375 g   (c) 5400 g   (d) 336 g   (e) 504 g   (f) 168 g

'Challenge' answers (using calculator and more accurate conversions)

2 Allow answers that are 'correct' but in either m, cm or mm
   (a) 17.78 cm   (b) 25.4 cm   (c) 91.44 cm   (d) 2.7432 m   (e) 45.72 cm
   (f) 10.0584 m (g) 4.572 cm   (h) 91.44 m   (i) 1.8288 m

3 Allow answers that are correctly expressed in ml
   (a) 22.73 litres   (b) 81.828 litres   (c) 227.3 litres   (d) 3.976 litres
   (e) 6.816 litres   (f) 13.632 litres

4 Allow answers that are correctly expressed in g or kg
   (a) 2.268 kg   (b) 3.402 kg   (c) 5.4432 kg (d) 340.2 g   (e) 510.3 g   (f) 170.1 g

Unit M6/1 Length, mass and capacity

1   Complete these conversions:

   (a) $\frac{7}{10}$ kg = ... g   (b) $\frac{2}{5}$ l = ... ml   (c) $\frac{9}{10}$ m = ... mm

   (d)   5365 ml = ... l   (e) $\frac{3}{4}$ m = ... mm   (f)   8205 g = ... kg

   (g)   7 mm = ... cm   (h) $2\frac{3}{4}$ kg = ... g   (i) $\frac{1}{4}$ l = ... ml

Many older people prefer to use the old *Imperial* units of measurement.

Here are some *approximate* conversions; they are not exact but can be used without a calculator!

Length: 1 inch is about $2\frac{1}{2}$ cm. 1 foot (12 inches) is about 30 cm. 1 yard (3 feet) is about 1 m 9 cm.

Weight: 1 pound (symbol: lb) is about 450 g, just under $\frac{1}{2}$ kg. 1 ounce (symbol: oz) is about 28 g.

Volume: 1 gallon (8 pints) is about $4\frac{1}{2}$ litres. 1 pint is just over $\frac{1}{2}$ a litre.

M6/1

2   Use these approximate conversions to change these into metric units of length:

   (a)   7 inches = ...   (b)   10 inches = ...   (c)   3 feet = ...

   (d)   9 feet = ...   (e)   1 foot, 6 inches = ...   (f)   11 yards = ...

   (g)   5 yards = ...   (h)   100 yards = ...   (i)   6 feet = ...

3   Use these approximate conversions to change these into metric units of volume:

   (a)   5 gallons = ...   (b)   18 gallons = ...   (c)   50 gallons = ...

   (d)   7 pints = ...   (e)   12 pints = ...   (f)   24 pints = ...

4   Use these approximate conversions to change these into metric units of weight:

   (a)   5 lb = ...   (b) $7\frac{1}{2}$ lb = ...   (c)   12 lb = ...

   (d)   12 oz = ...   (e)   18 oz = ...   (f)   6 oz = ...

Challenge

Use a calculator and these figures to make more accurate conversions:

Length: 1 inch = 2.54 cm   1 foot = 0.3048 m   1 yard = 0.9144 m

Volume: 1 pint = 0.568 litres   1 gallon = 4.546 litres

Weight: 1 ounce = 28.35 g   1 lb = 0.4536 kg

Now you know why the less accurate conversions are easier!

Unit M6/2 Area and perimeter using formulas

PNS Framework objective

- Calculate the perimeter and area of rectilinear shapes; estimate the area of an irregular shape by counting squares.

Unit learning outcome

- To calculate areas and perimeters of rectangles using formulae.

Prior knowledge

- Familiar with units of length and can envisage approximately how large they are.
- Knows that flat, two-dimensional space is referred to as 'area' and can be measured in square units with a ^{2} symbol placed after the linear unit to denote that it is a square unit.

Starter activities

- Ask the children to estimate a body measurement (e.g. a finger tip) that is approximately the same as a centimetre. Check with rulers and see if everyone has the same body measurement in cm (e.g. does everyone's little finger tip measure 1 cm wide or deep?) With the aid of metre sticks challenge them to find a body measurement approximately equal to a metre in length. (Hint: they can measure from outstretched arms to another part of their standing-up body.)
- Introduce the idea of measuring in square units. Make a metre square (tape four metre sticks together) and compare it with a square centimetre. Which would be better for measuring the area of a book, the floor, etc.?

Answers to M6/2

		Area	Perimeter
1	(a)	35 cm^2	24 cm
	(b)	175 m^2	64 m
	(c)	600 mm^2	100 mm
	(d)	512 cm^2	96 cm
	(e)	1500 m^2	160 m
	(f)	3 m^2	7 m
	(g)	27 m^2	21 m
	(h)	5400 cm^2	300 cm
2	Open answers		

Unit M6/2 Area and perimeter using formulas

Area is the amount of flat (two-dimensional) space which something occupies.

We use 'square' units to measure area, such as square metres (m²) and square centimetres (cm²).

To find the area of a rectangle, use the formula *area = length × breadth*.

So for this rectangle *6 cm × 4 cm* = an area of *24 cm²*.

Perimeter is the distance all the way around, so to find the perimeter of this rectangle, use the formula *perimeter = (length + width) × 2*:

$\qquad$ *(6 cm + 4 cm) × 2 [= 10 cm × 2] = 20 cm.*

6 cm
4 cm

M6/2

1   Find the area and perimeter of these rectangles; take care with the units of measure, they are not all in cm.

		Area	Perimeter
(a)	An oblong 5 cm wide and 7 cm long	....	....
(b)	A playground 25 m long and 7 m wide	....	....
(c)	A sticker 30 mm × 20 mm	....	....
(d)	An envelope 32 cm × 16 cm	....	....
(e)	A car park 50 m × 30 m	....	....
(f)	A painting 2 m wide and 1½ m tall	....	....
(g)	A flowerbed 6 m long and 4½ m wide	....	....
(h)	A table top 90 cm wide and 60 cm deep	....	....

2   Draw two different rectangles below each with a perimeter of 16 cm. Write the area in the centre of each rectangle.

Challenge

Can you adapt the perimeter formula to work out the length and breadth of rectangles with the same perimeter?

How many different rectangles could you draw with a perimeter of 30 cm? What is the area of each one?

Unit M6/3 Area and perimeter using partitioning

PNS Framework objective

- Calculate the perimeter and area of rectilinear shapes; estimate the area of an irregular shape by counting squares.

Unit learning outcome

- To calculate the areas and perimeters of shapes by dissecting into rectangles and triangles.

Prior knowledge

- Able to work out the area of rectangles by multiplication.

Starter activity

- In pairs ask children to draw and cut out three rectangles measuring 10 cm × 5 cm. Cut two of them in half diagonally and put all five pieces together to make a shape. Ask them to draw their shape on squared paper. Compare the shapes – do any look like anything in particular? Next ask them to draw two 5 cm × 5 cm squares and cut one of these in two diagonally. Make a new shape using all eight pieces and draw it. Compare drawings. Do any look like anything? Point out that all the shapes have the same area as they all started with the same squares and rectangles.

Answers to M6/3

1 17.5 cm²	**2** 12 cm²	**3** 16 cm²	**4** 15 cm²	**5** 7 cm²
6 27 cm²	**7** 27 cm²	**8** 40 cm²	**9** 47 cm²	**10** 14 cm²

Unit M6/3 Area and perimeter using partitioning

We can find the area of some shapes by partitioning them into rectangles and right-angled triangles.

Remember, to find the area of a right-angled triangle multiply the two shorter sides and divide by 2.

This trapezium can be split into a 5 cm × 3 cm rectangle and a right-angled triangle with the two shorter sides 2 cm and 3 cm.

The 2 cm side was found by subtracting the shorter side of the trapezium from the longer side.

The area of this trapezium is: 5 cm × 3 cm + (3 cm × 2 cm) ÷ 2, = *18 cm²*.

M6/3

Work out the area of these shapes by dividing them into rectangles and right-angled triangles.

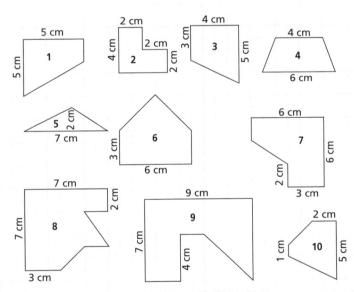

Each square of the grid represents 1 cm

shape 1 = ...   shape 2 = ...   shape 3 = ...   shape 4 = ...

shape 5 = ...   shape 6 = ...   shape 7 = ...   shape 8 = ...

shape 9 = ...   shape 10 = ...

Challenge

Use squared paper to draw a similar shape of your own. Ask a partner if they can work out the area while you try to do theirs.

Unit D5/1 What's the chance?

PNS Framework objective

- Describe the occurrence of familiar events using the language of chance or likelihood.

Unit learning outcome

- To consider probability of events happening.

Prior knowledge

- Understands the terms 'possible', 'impossible', 'unlikely', 'even chance' and 'certain'.
- Able to work out graphically what are the possible outcomes of dice throwing.

Starter activity

- Brainstorm things that are 'certain' to happen today. Challenge suggestions – are they absolutely certain or just almost certain? Make a similar list of things that definitely won't happen today; discuss the suggestions – could some be *just possible*? Decide if any are *'possible but unlikely'*. Talk about things that have an even chance of happening and be prepared to challenge suggestions, e.g. 'A boy will be the first to come in from playtime' – are there equal numbers of boys and girls? Use a probability scale line on the whiteboard (as per the one on the worksheet) and use labelled arrows to mark how close the near-impossible and near-certain events are to the two extremes of the scale. Have a bit of fun with the suggestions!

Answers to D5/1

1	(a) Even	(b) Unlikely or possible	(c) Impossible
2	(a) Unlikely or possible	(b) Unlikely or possible	(c) Unlikely or possible
	(d) Impossible	(e) 7	

3 and **4** Answers will vary

Unit D5/1 What's the chance?

If we toss a coin up into the air:
- it is *certain* that the coin will fall downwards
- it is *unlikely* that it will land on its edge
- there is an *even chance* that it will land 'heads' uppermost
- and *impossible* that it will float around in the air!

We use words and phrases such as these to make predictions about how events may turn out:

impossible, possible, unlikely, even chance, likely, certain

Choose from these words to answer the questions.

D5/1

1   If you throw a dice, what is the chance of throwing:

   (a) an odd number? ......   (b) a 6? ......   (c) an 8? ......

2   If you throw 2 dice and total them, what is the chance of throwing a total score of:

   (a) 2? .... (b) 4? .... (c) 7? .... (d) 14? ....

   (e) Which of these scores has the highest probability? ....

   The hardest predictions to make are those that are so unlikely that we think they are impossible, and those that are so likely that we think they are certain.

3   Try these:

   (a) You will go home today ....   (b) Your teacher will buy you an ice cream ....

   (c) It will be a wet playtime ....   (d) You will ask for extra homework ....

   (e) You will eat bread today ....   (f) A boy will be the first person to line up ....

   (g) You will have a drink today ....   (h) You will become Prime Minister one day .....

   (i) You will eat fish today ....   (j) Someone will fall over at playtime ....

   (k) You will watch TV tonight ....   (l) You will walk to school tomorrow ....

4   Draw the letters **a** to **l** on the scale line below to show how likely the events in question 3 are.

             less likely | *more likely*

   chance   even chance   certain

Challenge

Make up some events of your own and use words and a scale line to predict the chances.

Unit D5/2 Bar charts

PNS Framework objective

- Construct frequency tables, pictograms and bar and line graphs to represent the frequencies of events and changes over time.

Unit learning outcome

- To construct and interpret bar charts.

Prior knowledge

- Able to use tallying to carry out an investigation.

Starter activity

- Ask the children (possibly in pairs) to try and make a cube out of plasticine. Next ask them to use a pencil point (or alternative) to add indented dots to make it into dice. Let them roll them a few times and tally the outcome. Does anyone have one which is clearly biased to one or two outcomes? Examine its shape, edges and corners. Compare it with one that appears to be a fairer dice and with a manufactured dice – the shape needs to be regular and the edges and corners uniform to make it 'fair'. Some cheats use 'loaded' dice that are weighted inside to make them land with a particular face upwards.

Answers to D5/2

1 (a)

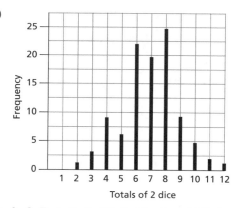

(b) 8, 6, 7, 4, 9, 5, 10, 3, 11, 2 and 12, 1

(c)

Total score	2	3	4	5	6	7	8	9	10	11	12
Possibilities	1	1	2	2	3	3	3	2	2	1	1

(d) It's not possible to score less than 2 with two dice

2 Answers will vary

Unit D5/2 Bar charts

1   Greg and Rachel have thrown 2 dice 100 times and have counted the frequency of each
    total score.

    (a)   Complete the bar graph:

Total	Frequency
1	0
2	1
3	3
4	9
5	6
6	22
7	20
8	25
9	7
10	5
11	2
12	1

Totals of 2 dice thrown 100 times

    (b)   List the scores in *descending* order of frequency (starting with the highest)

    ....

    (c)   How many possible ways are there to make each total score?

Total score	2	3	4	5	6	7	8	9	10	11	12
Number of possibilities	1										1

    (d)   Explain why there is no score of 1 ....

2   With a partner complete your own survey by throwing a pair of dice *60* times.
    Tally then add up the frequency of each score in the table below, then complete the bar
    graph.

Total	Tally	Frequency
1		
2		
3		
4		
5		
6		
7		
8		
9		
10		
11		
12		

Totals of 2 dice thrown 60 times

Challenge

Use your results to predict what the frequencies *might be* if you threw the dice another
60 times. Carry out another 60 throws and see how close your predictions were.

D5/2

Unit D5/3 Venn and Carroll diagrams

PNS Framework objective

- Answer a set of related questions by collecting, selecting and organising relevant data; draw conclusions, using ICT to present features, and identify further questions to ask.

Unit learning outcome

- To construct and interpret a Venn diagram (three criteria) and to construct and interpret Carroll diagrams.

Prior knowledge

- Firm grasp of what a 'set' is.
- Can understand the properties of sectors where sets overlap.

Starter activity

- Draw a set of three intersecting Venn rings on the whiteboard and label each with a 'likes...' statement. Ask the children which sector they would belong in. Ascertain if there is anyone who does not belong inside any of the rings. Place a number on each of seven tables in the room.

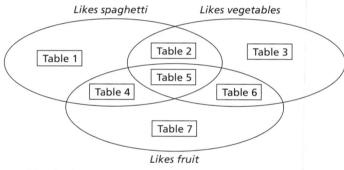

Explain that in order to save space on the diagram you are simply going to assign a table to each sector. Mark these on your Venn diagram.

Ask the children to go and sit around the table that matches their sector of the diagram. Anyone who does not fit inside any of the rings remains standing by the whiteboard. Change the criteria for the rings and again ask children to move to the correct table. Check that they know the specific criteria for the table they have sat at. Invite a volunteer to nominate labels for the Venn rings.

Answers to D5/3

1 (a) Greg doesn't collect things　　(b) Chantel doesn't collect or make anything
(c) Richard doesn't collect things and does not take part in sport
(d) Ian's group collect things,　　　　Peggy's group collect things and take part in sport,
Chantel's group take part in sport,　　Niamh's group collect and make things,
Catrina's group collect and make things and take part in sport,
Siobhan's group make things and take part in sport
Amarprit's group make things,　　　Amanda's group don't do any of these activities
2 (a) 5　　(b) 20　　(c) 11　　(d) 9　　(e) Amarprit, Rachel, Douglas and Siobhan
(f) Amanda　　(g) Answers will vary

Unit D5/3 Venn and Carroll diagrams

1   Here is a Venn diagram that shows children who have hobbies. Each ring is labelled to tell us about the people inside it.

People can be inside more than one ring, or, like Patrick, may not be in any.

The names appear in 8 groups.

Collecting things   *Active in sport*

Ian   Peggy   Chantel
Douglas
Joseph   John   Dougal
Poppy   Catrina   Ibrahim
Naimh   Vicky   Siobhan
William   Greg
Amarprit   Rachel   Amanda
Philip   Richard   Patrick

Making things

(a)   What doesn't Greg do? ....

(b)   What doesn't Chantel do? ....

(c)   What doesn't Richard do? ....

(d)   What do the members of each group do?

Ian's group ....   Peggy's group ....

Chantel's group ....   Niamh's group ....

Catrina's group ....   Siobhan's group ....

Amarprit's group ....   Amanda's group ....

D5/3

2   This is a *Carroll* diagram, named after Lewis Carroll, writer of the famous 'Alice' books.

The children are in columns according to their year group and rows according to what they do at dinner time.

	Year 4	Year 5	Year 6
Has school dinners	Amarprit Rachel Douglas Siobhan	Philip Richard Lesley	Christopher Vicky Joseph Patrick
Has packed lunch	Chantel Greg	Dougal Ibrahim Hayley Luke	Niamh Poppy Peggy
Goes home for dinner	Catrina Ian	Amanda	John William

(a) How many go home for dinner? ....   (b) How many stay in school at dinner time? ....

(c) How many have a school dinner? ....   (d) How many have a packed lunch? ....

(e) Which Year 4 children have school dinners? ....

(f) Who goes home from Year 5? ....

(g) Put the names of some of your class into this Carroll diagram.

	Boy	Girl
Dark hair		
Light hair		

Challenge

Make up another Carroll diagram, choosing how you sort the information for the columns and rows.

Unit D5/4 Mode, median and mean

PNS Framework objective

- Find and interpret the mode of a set of data.

Unit learning outcome

- To find the mode, median and mean of a set of data.

Prior knowledge

- Able to add lists of numbers and divide them using a calculator.
- Able to order a set of numbers.

Starter activity

- 'Calculator race': Give everyone (or pairs) a calculator and ask them to add a sequence of five numbers as you call them out, then put up hands to give you the total. Anyone who gives the wrong answer drops out. Start by pausing between the numbers; but increase the pace with each successive set. As more children drop out mix in some larger numbers.

Answers to D5/4

1. (a) The Reading test   mean: 25   median: 25   mode: 24
   (b) The Writing test   mean: 27   median: 27   mode: 28
   (c) The Spelling test   mean: 17   median: 18   mode: 20
   (d) Maths test 'A'   mean: 28   median: 29.5   mode: 33
   (e) Maths test 'B'   mean: 28   median: 30.5   mode: no mode
   (f) The Mental Maths test   mean: 12   median: 12   mode: 12
   (g) Science test 'A'   mean: 32   median: 30   mode: 29
   (h) Science test 'B'   mean: 30   median: 29   mode: 28
2. (a) Drew, Joseph, Niamh, Patrick, Poppy and William
   (b) Drew, Joseph, Niamh and William
   (c) No one scored higher than the mode
3. Answers will vary

Unit D5/4 Mode, median and mean

The Year 6 children have just spent a week doing SATs practice tests. Here are their scores.

	English Reading	Writing	Spelling	Maths test 'A'	Maths test 'B'	Mental Maths	Science test 'A'	Science test 'B'
Chris	15	28	17	38	32	12	29	28
Drew	35	36	19	33	33	13	29	30
Jon	8	14	7	15	12	5	20	18
Joseph	33	35	20	28	30	15	41	42
Niamh	29	32	20	36	37	12	31	28
Patrick	24	21	18	19	18	7	22	22
Peggy	26	28	15	33	31	14	29	25
Poppy	24	25	18	25	25	12	40	37
Vicky	24	23	16	31	35	18	43	39
William	32	28	20	22	27	12	36	31

There are different ways to compare data like this.

To find the *mean* add up all the scores and divide by the number of scores

Example: the Reading test score total is 250 and there are 10 children's scores, so the Reading test mean is 250 ÷ 10 = 25.

The **mode**: simply find the **mo**st common score. The Reading test *mode* is 24 because that is the most common score.

The **median** is the **mid**dle score when the scores are put in order. If there are two middle scores add them together and halve the result. To find the median for the Reading test add the two middle numbers (26 + 29 = 55) and halve the result: 55 ÷ 2 = 27½.

1 Find the mean, median and mode of:

  (a) The Reading test: mean ....   median ....   mode ....

  (b) The Writing test: mean ....   median ....   mode ....

  (c) The Spelling test   mean ....   median ....   mode ....

  (d) Maths test 'A'   mean ....   median ....   mode ....

  (e) Maths test 'B'   mean ....   median ....   mode ....

  (f) The Mental Maths test   mean ....   median ....   mode ....

  (g) Science test 'A'   mean ....   median ....   mode ....

  (h) Science test 'B'   mean ....   median ....   mode ....

2 In the Spelling test, which children scored higher than:

  (a) The mean? ....

  (b) The median? ....

  (c) The mode? ....

3 Which of these three methods do you think works best? ....

Challenge

Add together the scores for both Science tests to find the overall mean, median and mode for Science.

Unit D6/1 Probability

PNS Framework objective

- Describe and predict outcomes from data using the language of chance or likelihood.

Unit learning outcome

- To classify events according to likelihood on a scale of 0 to 1.

Prior knowledge

- Understands the notion of probability and knows that some events are either impossible or certain while others have an even chance of happening.

Starter activity

- Brainstorm things that are certain or almost certain to happen today. Discuss which will definitely happen rather than very likely. Similarly, brainstorm events that are impossible or extremely unlikely to happen today and discuss which are definitely impossible. Play 'devil's advocate' and suggest circumstances in which events *might* or *might not* happen. Ask pairs of children to make up and write down an event that definitely will happen today, one that definitely won't, one that is most likely today and one that almost certainly won't. Discuss suggestions from several pairs.

Answers to D6/1

Answers will vary; but could inspire some interesting discussions!

Unit D6/1 Probability

Probability is a way of looking at how likely things are to happen. If you toss a coin it is equally likely to land as 'heads' or 'tails'.

To help us to estimate what the probability is we can use a scale of 0 to 1 like this:

```
             ½
0 _____ 1
Impossible    Evens     Certain
```

If an event is impossible we mark it on the scale at 0, if it is certain we mark it on as 1.

An even chance, such as the toss of a coin, is marked on as ½. Events that are possible but have a chance less or more than evens have to be *estimated* like this:

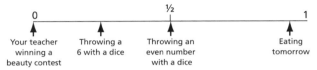

```
        0              ½              1
        ▲       ▲      ▲              ▲
   Your teacher   Throwing a  Throwing an      Eating
   winning a    6 with a dice  even number   tomorrow
   beauty contest          with a dice
```

D6/1

Estimate the probability of these things happening by putting a mark on each scale.

1 The sun will rise tomorrow.

   0 ½ 1

2 A boy will be the first to line up after playtime.

   0 ½ 1

3 You will be sent home early.

   0 ½ 1

4 There will be a school 'assembly' next Tuesday.

   0 ½ 1

5 Your teacher will smile at you.

   0 ½ 1

6 Tonight you will be kidnapped by aliens.

   0 ½ 1

7 It will rain today.

   0 ½ 1

8 A girl will be the first one ready at home time.

   0 ½ 1

9 Someone will fall over at playtime.

   0 ½ 1

10 You will play for a school sports team.

   0 ½ 1

11 You will watch television tonight.

   0 ½ 1

12 You will be given homework today.

   0 ½ 1

13 You will walk to school tomorrow.

   0 ½ 1

14 You will wash your teacher's car.

   0 ½ 1

15 You will eat fish today.

   0 ½ 1

16 You will have a birthday during this year.

   0 ½ 1

17 You will be 15 next birthday.

   0 ½ 1

18 You will go on holiday this year.

   0 ½ 1

19 You will have a drink today.

   0 ½ 1

20 You will eat Christmas cake today.

   0 ½ 1

Challenge

Make your own probability scale and write four events on it.

Unit D6/2 Line graphs

PNS Framework objective

- Construct and interpret frequency tables, bar charts with grouped discrete data, and line graphs; interpret pie charts.

Unit learning outcome

- To construct and interpret a line graph and investigate simple mappings on the graph.

Prior knowledge

- Able to plot positions on the graph and read off from one axis scale to the other.

Starter activity

- Draw a data table on the whiteboard showing hypothetical temperatures in the classroom at hourly intervals. Ask a few questions relating to the measured hourly readings. Then ask the children what temperature it was at an intermediate time (e.g. half-past 10). Can we be sure about that? What if someone left the door open during break time? Was it measured or have you *estimated* it? How did you reach that estimate? Would estimates closer to the o'clock times be more accurate than at half-past?

Answers to D6/2

1 (a) 16° C, M   (b) 14:00, 24°C, M   (c) 08:00, 10°C, M   (d) 22°C, E
   (e) Between 11:00 and 12:00, E   (f) After 14:00, E   (g) 08:00 to 10:00, M

2 (a) and (b)

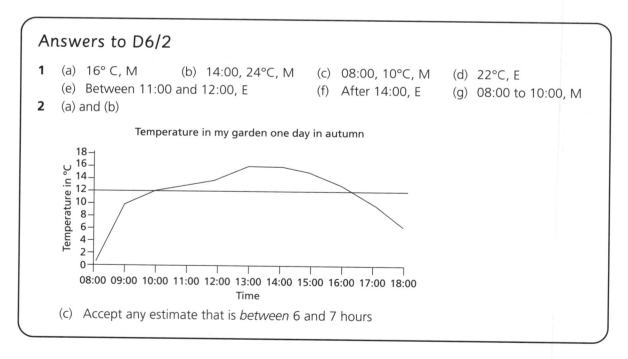

Temperature in my garden one day in autumn

(c) Accept any estimate that is *between* 6 and 7 hours

Unit D6/2 Line graphs

A keen weather watcher has taken temperature readings, has marked them on a graph and has joined up the points to make this *line graph*. We know that the temperature at the marked points is accurate; but between them we can only estimate.

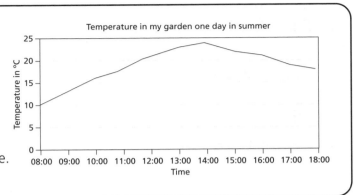

Temperature in my garden one day in summer

1 Use the graph to answer these questions. Put an *E* next to the answers that are estimates and an *M* by temperatures that were measured.

(a) What is the temperature at 10:00? ....

(b) When was the hottest temperature? .... What was it? ....

(c) When was the coldest temperature? .... What was it? ....

(d) What is the temperature at 12:30? ....

(e) About what time did the temperature rise above 20°C? ....

(f) When did the temperature begin to cool? ....

(g) Which 2-hour period had the fastest rise in temperature? ....

2 (a) Use this data to draw his graph for one day in autumn.

Time	08:00	09:00	10:00	11:00	12:00	13:00	14:00	15:00	16:00	17:00	18:00
Temperature	5°C	10°C	12°C	13°C	14°C	16°C	16°C	15°C	13°C	10°C	6°C

(b) Draw a line across the graph to show 12°C.

(c) How long does the temperature stay above 12°C?

Temperature in my garden one day in autumn

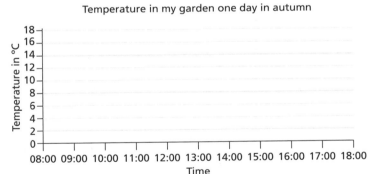

Challenge

Make up five questions that could be answered by looking at your graph and work out the answers.

Swap questions with a partner and test each other.

Unit D6/3 Conversion graphs

PNS Framework objective

- Construct and interpret frequency tables, bar charts with grouped discrete data, and line graphs; interpret pie charts.

Unit learning outcome

- To construct and interpret a conversion graph.

Prior knowledge

- Able to use a ruler perpendicular to one axis up to the straight line graph and read off the corresponding value on the other axis.
- Able to plot a position on the chart.

Starter activity

- Ask children approximately how long is 12 inches in cm? When they've found the answer ask for further approximations, starting with 6 and 24 inches then more difficult ones. Introduce an easy solution: draw a graph on the whiteboard (or better still have one already prepared) that has cm on the x-axis 0 to 100 and inches on the y-axis 0 to 40. Mark a cross where 30 cm intersects with 12 inches and draw a line from (0, 0) right through it to the end of the scales. Demonstrate how to use a ruler to go from the inches scale across to the line then down to the cm scale to convert inches to cm. Show how to convert cm to inches. Ask volunteers to make conversions using the chart.

Answers to D6/3

1. (a) 1.1 lb (b) 1.4 lb (c) 0.7 kg (d) 6.6 lb (e) 5.5 lb (f) 3.6 kg
   (g) 7.7 lb (h) 1.8 kg (i) 2.3 kg (j) 1.1 kg (k) 1.8 lb (l) 3.4 kg
2. Check that the line is correctly drawn from (0, 0) to (16, 10), the scales have been completed and there is an appropriate title on the chart
3. (a) 4.58 km (b) 3.1 miles (c) 9.6 km (d) 9.4 miles
   (e) 2.3 miles (f) 6.4 km (g) 5 miles (h) 12.8 km

Unit D6/3 Conversion graphs

We can use *straight line graphs* for quickly making approximate conversions if we know that one unit of measure equals another.

The graph on the right is an easy way to approximately convert weights given in kg to pounds, and weights given in pounds to kg. It uses the rounded conversion formula: 1 kg = 2.2 lb (pounds).

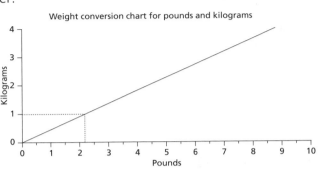

Weight conversion chart for pounds and kilograms

D6/3

1   Use a ruler to make these conversions:

   (a) 0.5 kg = ... lb   (b) 3 lb = ... kg   (c) 1.5 lb = ... kg

   (d) 3 kg = ... lb   (e) 2.5 kg = ... lb   (f) 8 lb = ... kg

   (g) 3.5 kg = ... lb   (h) 4 lb = ... kg   (i) 5 lb = ... kg

   (j) 2.5 lb = ... kg   (k) 0.8 kg = ... lb   (l) 7.5 lb = ... kg

2   Make a distance conversion chart for miles and kilometres.
    Complete the scales.
    Mark a cross where 10 miles intersects with 16 kilometres.
    Draw a straight line joining this cross to (0, 0).
    Give the chart a title.

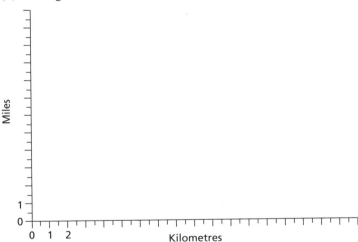

3   Use your chart to make these conversions:

   (a) 3 miles = ... km   (b) 5 km = ... miles   (c) 6 miles = ... km

   (d) 15 km = ... miles   (e) 4 km = ... miles   (f) 4 miles = ... km

   (g) 8 km= .... miles   (h) 8 miles = ... km

Challenge

Make a conversion chart for gallons and litres using the rounded formula:

2 gallons = 9 litres

Make up some conversion problems of your own.

Unit D6/4 Frequency tables and bar charts

PNS Framework objective

- Construct and interpret frequency tables, bar charts with grouped discrete data, and line graphs; interpret pie charts.

Unit learning outcome

- To use frequency tables and bar graphs with grouped data.

Prior knowledge

- Able to count up how many scores fall within each data range.
- Able to draw a bar graph.

Starter activity

- Make a tally chart to show how many of the children and adults in the room were born in each month of the year. Announce that you are going to group the months together to make a bar graph to show how many were born in spring, summer, autumn and winter. Make a grouped data table with labels: March to May (spring); June to August (summer); September to November (autumn); and December to February (winter). Use this to make a bar chart.

Answers to D6/4

1

Score groups	Spelling	Maths
30	3	2
26–29	5	6
21–25	6	7
16–20	4	4
10–15	3	3
< 10	4	3

2 (a) 18   (b) 19
3 (a) 7   (b) 6

4

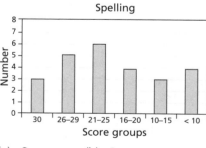

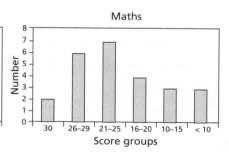

5 (a) 8   (b) 8
6 (a) 21–25   (b) 30 and the 10–15 group

Unit D6/4 Frequency tables and bar charts

Everyone in Class 6 at Rowland Junior School has had two tests, both marked out of 30.

	Alan	Alison	Amanda	Amarprit	Andy	Carol	Chris	Christopher	Craig	Greg	Ibrahim	Jenny	John	Jon	Joseph	Lesley	Niamh	Pam	Patrick	Paul	Peggy	Poppy	Rachel	Vicky	William
Spelling	25	30	18	19	27	13	22	20	30	21	26	28	30	21	11	13	23	7	23	29	17	5	29	8	5
Maths	28	25	26	24	29	14	25	17	24	16	30	30	29	26	8	26	25	9	25	16	14	6	24	12	17

To see how well the class as a whole are doing, we can put the scores together into groups. This is called *grouped data*.

D6/4

1   Complete the grouped data table on the right.

2   How many children scored more than half:

(a)   in spelling? ....   (b)   in maths? ....

3   How many children scored less than half:

(a)   in spelling? ....   (b)   in maths? ....

Score groups	Spelling	Maths
30	3	
26 → 29	5	
21 → 25		7
16 → 20		
10 → 15		
< 10		3

4   Complete these graphs:

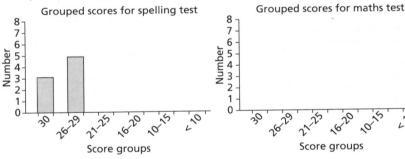

Grouped scores for spelling test

Grouped scores for maths test

5   How many children scored 26 or more:

(a)   in spelling? ....   (b)   in maths? ....

6   Look at the grouped data table in question 1.

(a)   Which score group has most children? ....

(b)   Which score groups have fewest children? ....

Challenge

How would you group the scores?

Regroup the scores and draw new graphs.

Do the graphs based on your groupings make the class's results look any different?

Unit D6/5 Mean, mode, median and range

PNS Framework objective

- Describe and interpret results and solutions to problems using the mode, range, median and mean.

Unit learning outcome

- To find the range and different averages of a set of data.

Prior knowledge

- Understands that data is numerical information which has been collected for further study.

Starter activity

- On the whiteboard write down the children's names and the number of siblings each has. Which number of siblings appears most? Identify this number as being the mode, pointing out that mode and most begin with the same two letters. Write out the scores in ascending order and find the middle one. Identify this as the median, pointing out that 'median' and 'middle' both sound vaguely similar. If viable, work out the mean, adding up all the siblings and dividing by the number of children. Identify this as the mean, pointing out that sharing out could seem 'mean' for the children who end up with fewer siblings!

Answers to D6/5

1   24

2   (a) 22   (b) $22\frac{1}{2}$ (c) $23\frac{1}{2}$ (d) $22\frac{1}{3}$

3   (a)   6, 8, 9, 12, 14, 14, 16, 16, 17, 17, 24, 24, 24, 25, 25, 25, 25, 26, 26, 26, 28, 29, 29, 30, 30
    (b) 24   (c) 25

Unit D6/5 Mean, mode, median and range

You will need a calculator for this unit.

One way of examining data is to look at the range. The range is the difference between the highest and lowest score.

If you take 5 (the lowest spelling score) away from 30 (the highest score) you will find that the range of the spelling scores is 25.

	Alan	Alison	Amanda	Amarprit	Andy	Carol	Chris	Christopher	Craig	Greg	Ibrahim	Jenny	John	Jon	Joseph	Lesley	Niamh	Pam	Patrick	Paul	Peggy	Poppy	Rachel	Vicky	William
Spelling	25	30	18	19	27	13	22	20	30	21	26	28	30	21	11	13	23	7	23	29	17	5	29	8	5
Maths	28	25	26	24	29	14	25	17	24	16	30	30	29	26	8	26	25	9	25	16	14	6	24	12	17

1   What is the range for the maths test? ....

Another way to look at scores is to calculate the *mean* score.

To find the mean add up all the scores and divide by the number of scores.

To find the mean of all 25 maths scores add them all up and divide by 25:

*525 [total] ÷ 25 [number] = **21 [mean]***

2   Find the mean of:

(a)   the spelling scores of the first 6 children (Alan to Carol) ....

(b)   the spelling scores of the first 10 children (Alan to Greg) ....

(c)   the maths scores of the first 8 children (Alan to Christopher) ....

(d)   the maths scores for the middle 10 children (Craig to Pam) ....

Another way to look at a set of data is to find the *median* and the *mode*.

Here are the spelling scores written out in ascending order:

5 5 7 8 11 13 13 17 18 19 20 21 | 21 | 22 23 23 25 26 27 28 29 29 | 30 30 30 |

The median is
the middle score
(or is between the two
middle scores)

The mode is the
most common score

3   (a)   Write out the maths scores in order ....

(b)   What is the median for the maths results? ....

(c)   What is the mode for the maths results? ....

Challenge

Look at the scores of some of the children.

Choose a few of the children and work out the mean of both of their test scores.